THE GREAT ORME TRAMWAY

THE GREAT ORME TRAMWAY

– over a century of service

by

Keith Turner

ISBN: 0-86381-817-X

Cover design: Sian Parri

First published in 2003 by
Gwasg Carreg Gwalch, 12 Iard yr Orsaf, Llanrwst, Wales LL26 0EH
☎ 01492 642031   🖷 01492 641502

CONTENTS

INTRODUCTION

On Wednesday 31 July 2002 the Great Orme Tramway celebrated its centenary, one hundred years to the day after the first section of the line was opened to the public. Since that momentous day of a century ago this unique cable tramway has – give or take the occasional interruption – performed tirelessly its task of transporting residents and visitors up the Great Orme headland in the North Wales resort of Llandudno.

It has been more than a quarter of a century since I first rode on the tramway, and during the intervening years I have kept a keen eye on its fortunes. As during the preceding 75 years, those fortunes have, at times, been decidedly mixed; it is to be hoped though that this unique line is allowed to survive – and prosper – for another century of faithful service.

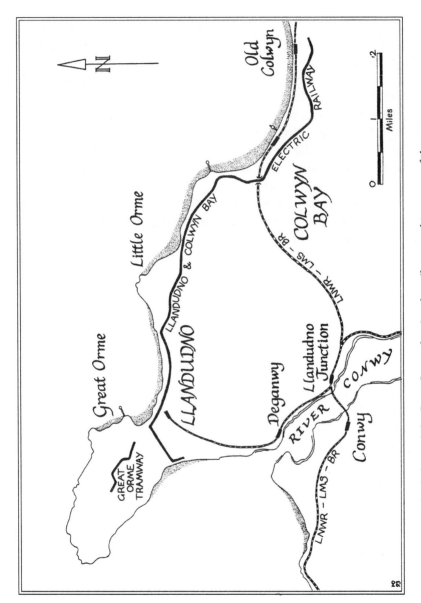

Llandudno and the Great Orme, showing the railways and tramways of the area.

Chapter One
LLANDUDNO AND THE ORME

The Great Orme – or Y Gogarth in Welsh – is without doubt the most distinctive feature of Llandudno; indeed, it once was its *only* distinctive feature before the modern town as it exists today was laid out. From the west, as far along the North Wales coast as Bangor, it appears to be a flat, off-shore island rising abruptly from the sea and it only gives lie to this illusion as one approaches nearer. The Orme, as it is usually referred to, consists of a limestone mass some two miles long and one mile wide, rising to 679ft above the sea from which it rears so steeply and spectacularly on three sides. This fanciful resemblance to the head of a half-submerged sea monster is believed to account for the origin of its name which derives from the Old Norse word *ormr* for (giant) worm or serpent, antecedent of the Old English *wyrm*. On its fourth, south-east side the Orme is connected to the mainland by a very low, very flat strip of land – the serpent's neck – that over the course of millennia has been alternatively submerged and exposed by the sea.

In pre-Roman times copper (and later lead) ore was mined on the Orme; extraction was continued by the Romans but apparently later abandoned, only to be revived at the end of the seventeenth century. Mining continued for roughly another century and a half on land leased from the Orme owners, the Bishop of Bangor and the Mostyn family (whose seat was at Gloddaeth near the Little Orme). The last copper mine to close, in 1855, was the Tŷ Gwyn mine located close to what is now the Marine Drive entrance to the pier. As will be seen, the end of mining in the town set in motion a chain of events leading almost directly to the construction of the Great Orme Tramway.

From at least the sixth century a building has stood, in a hollow a little to the north of the comparatively level summit, on the site of the present St Tudno's church. The church gave its name to the parish (Llandudno meaning the Parish, or Holy Place, of Tudno) and originally served the handful of miners' cottages huddled together on the landward side of the Orme. The structure of the present St Tudno's church dates back to the early fifteenth century, though it was heavily rebuilt in 1859; ironically, it lost its parish church status just three years later to St George's in Church Walks. It still served as the burial place of choice for many residents, however, and when, in 1903, the local council laid out its municipal cemetery, it sited it next to the old church.

As late as the mid-ninteenth century the miners' cottages and two small inns were the only habitations on the landward side of the peninsula, part of the Mostyn estate. All that was about to change, however, in a remarkable way: at very same time as copper mining was dying in Llandudno, North Wales was becoming 'tourist conscious' and the Mostyn family realised that the rise of the fashionable watering place need by no means be confined solely to the south coast of England; with this in mind they began a grand scheme, to not only build from scratch a complete resort, but to then elevate it to a position in the north equal to that occupied by Brighton in the south. In 1843 Edward, 1st Baron Mostyn, obtained an Enclosure Act (steered through Parliament by his son and heir, Edward Mostyn Lloyd-Mostyn, who was MP for Flintshire at the time) permitting him to develop the low-lying peninsula and accordingly, in 1849, he offered for sale 176 plots of building land at 6d (2.5p) a square yard on 99-year leases. The scheme had taken its first steps to becoming an unqualified success and so fulfilling all of Lord Mostyn's hopes.

Paradoxically, this development could only have taken place because Llandudno lost out to Holyhead in the 1840s in the competition to find a suitable railhead for the mail boat service to Ireland, thus preventing the hamlet from becoming the site a major port. It would appear that the idea for the resort scheme came from Lord Mostyn's estate agent, John Williams, who was also Secretary to the Tŷ Gwyn mining company and therefore in an excellent position to observe the declining fortunes of mining in the area.

From these humble beginnings sprang up the town that stands today, facing out to the east across the great curve of Ormes Bay bounded by the Great Orme on the left and its smaller namesake, the Little Orme, to the right. With its broad promenade and majestic sweep of hotels and boarding houses along the bay it followed rigidly the pattern of its day, but in one respect it was unique - and that one respect was without doubt one of the principal reasons behind Llandudno's success: behind the town was *another* beach – a longer, wider, more desolate stretch of sand bordering the Conwy estuary. This added attraction, together with the impressive majesty of the Great Orme, meant that Lord Mostyn's project could hardly fail: the town's population which had totalled just 1,131 in 1851 had risen to 4,193 thirty years later, and by 1891 it had grown by nearly half as much again to 6,065; ten years after that it had become an Urban District (principally by dint of absorbing the neighbouring Civil Parish of Eglwys Rhos) with a total of 9,279 inhabitants – a figure which could probably be safely doubled (or even tripled) any time during the summer months. In contrast, population figures for the rest of north-west Wales remained fairly static throughout this period.

Other landmark events of note that occurred during the latter half of the nineteenth century, both inextricably linked to the rise of Llandudno to its pre-eminent position among the resorts of the North Wales coast, were the connecting of the town to the national railway system in 1858, the opening of the present-day pier in 1877 (for visitors to take the air as well as to make use of steamer services to Liverpool and neighbouring resorts) and, in 1892, the opening of a new, five-platform railway station designed to cope with the summer influx of regular, special and excursion trains bringing their thousands of holiday-makers from the north-west of England, the Midlands and London. Indeed, by the time the pier opened in 1877 the town was already styled 'the Queen of Welsh watering-places' with, according to *The Gossiping Guide to Wales* published that year: 'Baths you can enjoy, native and Turkish – *al fresco* and enclosed [and] a splendid Hydropathic Establishment, admirably conducted, in the town, if you believe in water'.

So Llandudno grew, relying completely and utterly on its annual surfeit of holiday-makers to the total exclusion of any other major form of industry (apart from the necessary services provision.) Improvement schemes to add to the amenities of the town were rife and, naturally, the Orme figured largely in several. Walks and gardens were planned and executed on its lower south-

CHAPTER xxvii.

An Act for incorporating the Great Orme Tramways Company and for authorising the Company to make and maintain a Tramway and Tramroad from Llandudno to or near the summit of the Great Ormeshead in the county of Carnarvon. [23rd May 1898.]

A.D. 1898.

WHEREAS the making and maintaining of a tramway and tramroad from Llandudno to or near the summit of the Great Ormeshead in the county of Carnarvon would be of local and public advantage :

And whereas the persons in that behalf in this Act named with others are willing at their own expense to construct such tramway and tramroad if authorised by Parliament so to do and are desirous of being incorporated into a company with adequate powers for the purpose and it is expedient that they be incorporated and empowered accordingly as by this Act provided :

And whereas plans and sections showing the lines and levels of the tramway and tramroad authorised by this Act and also a book of reference containing the names of the owners and lessees or reputed owners and lessees and of the occupiers of the lands required or which may be taken for the purposes or under the powers of this Act were duly deposited with the clerk of the peace for the county of Carnarvon and are herein-after respectively referred to as the deposited plans sections and book of reference :

And whereas the objects of this Act cannot be attained without the authority of Parliament :

May it therefore please Your Majesty that it may be enacted and be it enacted by the Queen's most Excellent Majesty by and with the advice and consent of the Lords Spiritual and Temporal and

[*Price* 1s. 9d.] A 1

The title page of the GOT's authorising Act of Parliament.

east-facing slope, including the landscaping of the natural amphitheatre known as Happy Valley, overlooking the western end of Ormes Bay, where a variety of open-air events had been staged ever since the establishment of the modern town. (This parcel of land was donated to the town in 1887 by the 3rd Baron Mostyn, to commemorate Queen Victoria's Golden Jubilee of that year.)

THE MARINE DRIVE

In 1879 a toll road round the headland was completed for those visitors daring enough to walk or ride (anticlockwise from east to west) along a roadway that clung to the very edge of the rockface. Constructed at a cost of £14,000 and running for a distance of 4 miles 130yd the Marine Drive, as it was named, soon proved a most popular attraction, replacing as it did a precipitous track known as Cust's Path, constructed in 1856-58 by one Reginald Cust, a trustee of the Mostyn Estates. Even before work on the road had begun in earnest – the first sod was cut on 9 September 1875 – suggestions were being made to replace, or combine, it with a horse tramway. One such proposal came from the writer of a letter to the *Caernarvon & Denbigh Herald* of 21 August 1875 who claimed that the tram fare would be in the region of only 3d (1p), compared with the sum of 5s (25p) charged by the fly drivers who conveyed people round the Orme on the existing pathways.There, however, the idea rested – at least for the time being until after the road had been purchased for £10,500 in 1897 by the Urban District Council from its private owners, the Great Orme's Head Marine Drive Co Ltd.

By the time of the Council's purchase of the Marine Drive it had become evident that people prepared to pay to encircle the Orme would presumably also be prepared to pay to ascend it in comfort. (The only means of vehicular access was by way of a very steep and rough road.) This belief was given weight by the success – on a far grander scale – of two pioneering lines not so far distant: the Snaefell Mountain Tramway opened in 1895 on the Isle of Man to the north-west, and the Snowdon Mountain Tramroad opened in

1896 rather closer to home to the south. The project to construct a tramway up the Great Orme was about to take shape.

THE TELEGRAPH INN

Once the steep, landward slope of the Great Orme has been scaled, the headland reveals itself to be an undulating, turf-covered plateau that drops away sharply to the sea on its other three sides. Too exposed for human habitation of the usual kind, it has nevertheless provided a residence one of form or another since the 1820s when, during that decade, the Liverpool Docks Trustees installed a telegraph system along the coast between their port and Holyhead. At a number of prominent vantage points along the coast – including the summit of the Great Orme – telegraph stations were set up, each with two tall wooden masts with movable semaphore arms, in order to pass messages of ship sightings from Holyhead back to Liverpool.

The Great Orme station had its own, purpose-built keeper's cottage which continued in use as this line of communication was updated, first to the electric telegraph in the 1840s and then to a telephone link at the end of the century. By this latter date the keeper of the cottage, known variously as Telegraph House or Telegraph Inn, had a well-established sideline serving refreshments to visitors. Situated just a hundred yards or so west of the actual summit of the Orme, the Telegraph Inn was the obvious terminal point for any railway or tramway proposal to carry visitors up to the headland.

Chapter Two
A TRAMWAY IS PROMOTED

AUTHORISATION

The first funicular, or cable-worked, cliff railway in Britain had opened at Scarborough as early as 1875 and this line had soon been followed by others around the coast; by the end of 1893 no less than thirteen similar railways had been constructed in the British Isles as local promoters quickly realised the commercial potential offered by hitherto unproductive cliffs in their resorts. Not surprisingly, the idea was put forward of installing a similar type of line up the Great Orme after two proposals for a conventional electric tramway on to the headland had come to nothing. Both these schemes had been put to the Works Committee of Llandudno UDC, in September 1894 and December 1895, by a Chester mining engineer by the name of Henry Enfield Taylor. Both tramways were to have commenced by the entrance to the pier; the first required the trams to reverse part-way up the ascent to help cope with the slope and while the second plan removed this obstacle, both lines would still have ended some distance short of, and below, the summit of the Orme.

Nothing having come of Taylor's proposals, a number of local business men decided to band together to promote their own tramway scheme, this time to reach the summit. Accordingly, they engaged as consulting engineers Messrs Wood & Fowler of Liverpool whose recommendation was a funicular tramway, with this being worked in two separate sections since the total distance involved was too long for it to be safely worked as one line, yet too short to justify the capital outlay and expenditure for the adoption of any other form of working (such as using rack and pinion locomotives, as on the Snowdon line). Notwithstanding this, the projected line would still be longer than any funicular railway in Britain and – unique in Britain at that time – would follow the Continental practice of negotiating appreciable curves and changes of gradient in the track *en route*.

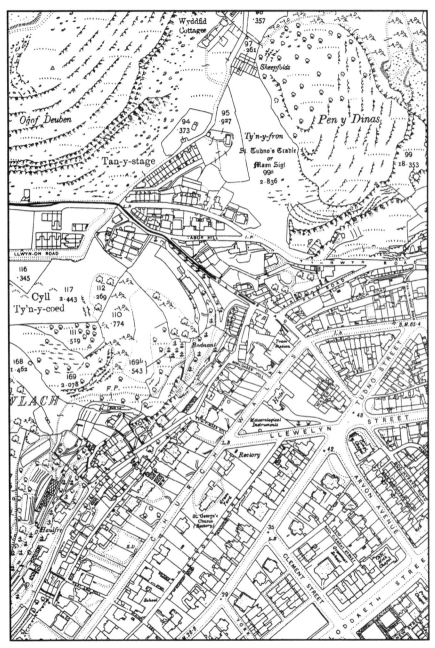

The lower section of the tramway, from Victoria Station to the passing loop in Tŷ Gwyn Road, as depicted on the Ordnance Survey 25in map of 1913.

The next important stage in the proceedings was to secure the necessary parliamentary approval for the scheme. Messrs R.S. Chamberlain & E.W. Johnson of Llandudno were engaged as solicitors to the group of promoters and the Great Orme Tramways Bill was accordingly drawn up and introduced in Parliament during the 1897-98 session. At a meeting of the Llandudno UDC in January 1898 the Council agreed not to offer any opposition to the passage of the Bill, the promoters having agreed to insert a special clause to afford it protection. Similar provision was made with respect to the Rt Hon Llewelyn Nevill Vaughan Baron Mostyn (the then Lord Mostyn), owner of the land over which the tramway would have to pass. The Bill had an uneventful journey through Parliament and received the Royal Assent on 23 May 1898, passing into law as the Great Orme Tramways Act. Its full title was:

An Act for incorporating the Great Orme Tramways Company and for authorising the Company to make and maintain a Tramway and Tramroad from Llandudno to or near the summit of the Great Ormeshead in the county of Carnarvon.

The authorisation had been given, according to the Act's preamble, because 'the making and maintaining of a tramway and tramroad... would be of local and public advantage'. The Great Orme Tramways Co was authorised by the Act to raise capital of £25,000 in £5 shares, with powers to borrow a further £6,250, and the number of directors was given as five (though the Company was permitted to alter this figure between the limits of three and seven). Qualification for a directorship was the holding of at least 40 shares and the initial directors listed in the Act were Richard Conway, John Jones, Stephen Dunphy, James Lanham Mayger and George Alfred Humphreys – all local residents and the scheme's original promoters. Conway was later appointed Chairman.

Permission was given to the Company by the Act to construct two sections of tramway, the first being a single line of 3 furlongs 6.00 chains (792yd) from a point in the yard behind the Victoria Hotel in Old Road, at its junction with Church Walks, up the Great Orme to a point near Penymynydd Uchaf farm house. The second tramway (described in the Act as a tramroad since it did not run along or beside a paved way) was to consist of a single line running 4 furlongs 0.80 chains (897.6yd) from the terminus of the first line to a point near the summit 110yd from the Telegraph Inn. The gauge of both lines was to be 3ft 6in and the rails, in the roadway sections, were to be laid level with the road surface. The rails were, in addition, to be of a type approved by the Board of Trade (which was also to inspect both sections of the line before they could be allowed to open). The time allowed for the compulsory purchase of the land needed was two years, with a further one year allowed for the completion of the works. The Company was specifically forbidden to take (ie demolish) more than ten houses belonging to the 'labouring class' – members of which being defined as earning under 30s (£1.50) a week.

Powers were given to erect a hotel at the summit of the Orme by the tramway terminus, on the Company's land, and also to erect offices, stations, waiting and refreshment rooms as need be. As regards the actual working of the line, this was left entirely up to the Company with any form of animal or mechanical power permitted, subject to the approval of the Board of Trade, with one important exception: steam working (ie with locomotives) was excluded from the possibilities, for the term 'mechanical power' was defined for the purposes of the Act as including 'electric and every other motive power not being steam or animal power'. If electric traction was adopted it was to be used with 'due regard to the telegraphic lines from time to time used or intended to be used by Her Majesty's Postmaster-General'. The Board of Trade was empowered to make any necessary byelaws to cover the use of mechanical power.

Other miscellaneous provisions were: the tramway was not to run on Sundays without the Council's consent; Old Road from the King's Head to the Iron Gate – the upper end of the roadway – was to be widened to at least 16ft by the Company; a passing place for vehicular traffic was to be built between Plas Road and Tabor Hill; for the protection of Lord Mostyn all tracks and roadways incorporated into, or destroyed by the construction of, the line had to be replaced after completion of the tramway, and all building plans had to be approved by him; and no rolling stock was to be used that had been constructed for railway use. Finally, there was a clause insisted upon by the Council which is a veritable classic of its kind:

The Company shall make provision for the conveyance at a reasonable and fixed charge and in a decent and seemly manner of corpses for internment in the St. Tudno Cemetery.

ENTER A RIVAL?

Even as the Great Orme Tramway was fast becoming a reality, the idea of a second tramway on the headland was undergoing serious consideration, this time by the Council. The proposal was that of a quarter of a century before, mentioned earlier, namely a tramway along the Marine Drive but this time using the now tried and tested power of electric traction. The reason for the resurrection of the idea is not hard to find: during the early 1890s a remarkably similar toll road had been constructed along the cliff face south of Douglas on the Isle of Man, and during 1896-97 an electric tramway some $3^{1}/_{4}$ miles in length had been opened along it for the benefit of tourists; this had been quickly followed by a funicular cliff railway at each end of the line. Douglas was a growing seaside resort closely resembling Llandudno, even down to the broad sweep of its promenade along a wide bay between two headlands, and with the two towns linked by steamship it is highly unlikely that any development designed to attract visitors to the Island went unnoticed in North Wales. Llandudno UDC accordingly commissioned an engineer, E. Paley Stephenson, to investigate the idea (which is thought to have originated in a private 1895 proposal for such a line as part of a larger Llandudno tramway system) and his report, submitted by the Council's General Purposes Committee to the whole Council in November 1901, was a detailed study for what would be known as the Great Orme's Head Marine Drive Tramway. This was to be a 3ft 6in gauge overhead electric tramway, the main section of which would occupy the entire length of the Marine Drive, from the Happy

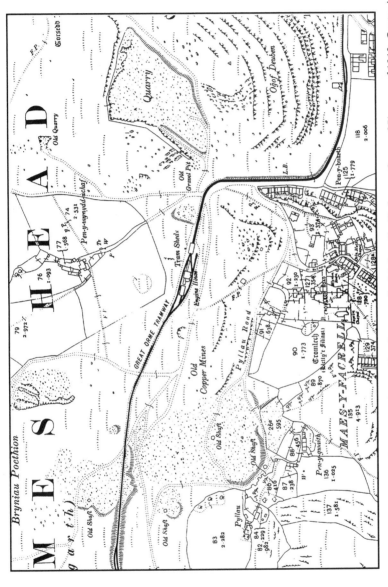

The tramway between the lower and upper section passing loops, as depicted on the Ordnance Survey 25in map of 1913. Centre is the pre-2001 complex of lower and upper section car sheds separated by the winding house. Note the storage siding, and the two tracks linking the sections, then still in use.

Valley Lodge on the eastern side of the Orme to the Penmorfa Lodge on the west, as a single track laid 3ft from the kerb on the landward side of the roadway. Between the two Marine Drive entrances – some $1^{1}/_{2}$ miles apart as the crow flies – a choice of two possible routes were considered. The first was via Abbey Road, West Parade, Conway Crescent, Gloddaeth Street and North Parade whilst the second was via Abbey Road, Tudnor Street, Church Walks and North Parade. The first route was the preferred one as a possible agreement could then be arranged with the promoters of a same-gauge electric tramway linking Llandudno and Colwyn Bay for common running over this section; the second route would be more costly to operate and, passing more houses, was also likely to raise more opposition from residents.

It was estimated that the construction of the line would entail the removal of about 1,350 cubic yards of rock from the Marine Drive as the road was discovered by Stephenson to be narrower than the statutory 16ft in several places. The cost of construction was estimated at £34,000 (adopting the first route) or £35,000 (for the second). The envisaged service would use both open and closed tramcars, running every 15 minutes in an anticlockwise direction round the Orme, with a fare of 6d (2.5p) being charged.

It is tempting to speculate as to whether or not the tramway would still be with us today if it had been built – but it was not, the scheme being defeated by a combination of opposition from local commercial interests, the disquiet expressed by residents alarmed at the cost, and the 'wait and see' approach adopted by the Council in respect of the fortunes of the two other lines then under construction, namely the Great Orme Tramway and the Llandudno & Colwyn Bay Electric Railway. Certainly, the troubled early years of the latter concern firmly discouraged the Council from becoming involved in the business of tramway operation, at least for the foreseeable future. As for its Manx counterpart across the Irish Sea, the Douglas Head Marine Drive Tramway, this was closed at the outbreak of World War II (as the Llandudno line would almost certainly have been) and was never reopened, a victim of the much-changed post-war social and economic climate.

CONSTRUCTION

Having expended some £4,000 on promotional expenses the newly-formed GOT Co was anxious to press ahead with raising its capital and acquiring the land needed. The process proved to be slow and quiet, though the *North Wales Chronicle* of 9 September 1899 mentioned that the Company had purchased the Telegraph Inn and the adjacent land at the summit for the purpose of erecting a 'good hotel' there. A year later all the necessary land had been bought but construction had had to be delayed due to the fact that insufficient capital had as yet been raised. In October 1900 the Company announced that it would still definitely go ahead with the scheme and by March of the following year only £4,000 was left to be subscribed. The Company again announced that it was pressing ahead and that, according to the *Chronicle*, the line was to be worked on the 'tail rope' principle with a 'gas station' powering each section. The lower section was to be operational all the year round while the upper section was to be worked during the summer season only. (The lower section was intended to serve the residential area on the lower slopes of the Orme as well as catering for holiday-makers.)

Construction of the line eventually commenced in April 1901, the contract for the work, worth £3,133 12s 3d (£3,133.61), having been awarded to Thomas & John Owen, a Llandudno firm of builders. (John Owen of this firm was one of the original promoters of the tramway and, together with Richard Conway, served on Llandudno UDC; this and the fact that the other promoters were all local and influential men accounts for why so little official opposition was offered to the scheme.) The construction work had actually been sub-contracted by the main contractors, Richard White & Sons of Widnes, who supplied the permanent way materials, winding gear and rolling stock; this contract was worth £8,075. (Whites had accumulated some recent experience of laying steeply-graded track, having supplied the permanent way materials for the Snowdon Mountain Tramroad.) The work was carried out under the supervision of White's engineer, Henry Enfield Taylor of Chester – the very same engineer who had failed only a few years earlier with his own tramway proposals. (As it transpired, this sub-contracting arrangement did not prove satisfactory and gave rise to a court action described later.) The construction as a whole was directed by Mr A.R. Ellison on behalf of the consulting engineers. The work began, logically enough, at the lower end of the route near the bottom of Old Road and advanced upwards. On 19 April the UDC agreed to close Old Road to vehicular traffic so that track laying could continue unimpeded in the narrow alleyway (for such was the state of the road at that time). Many of the labourers employed were slate quarrymen from the nearby Penrhyn Quarry, at Bethesda, who were caught in the middle of a protracted lock-out; since their dispute lasted from 1900 to 1903, they were presumably grateful for any work they could find.

The first snag was immediately encountered: Old Road was so narrow that the track would unavoidably foul the water and gas mains below the surface. The Company offered, in June, to pay £10 towards the £40 cost of new pipes, as well as removing and replacing the old ones, but in August the UDC stuck out for £20 – a very good bargain for the Council since the pipes were at the end of their useful life anyway! As previously stated, under the terms of the 1898 Act Old Road had to be widened to at least 16ft and a passing place for other vehicles provided between Plas Road and Tabor Hill not less than 18ft long and 10ft wide. These requirements carried out, the line of rails emerged from Old Road and entered Tŷ Gwyn Road in June 1901 at a point known as Black Gate, or the Iron Gate (after the gate across the road intended to keep livestock straying down from the Orme). Just below the halfway point on the lower section work on laying the track halted and all hopes of opening the lower section that summer were decisively dashed; the cable and rolling stock manufacturers were accordingly advised to delay delivery until the following year when the tramway would be in a better position to accommodate the equipment. More roadworks were required here: the road had to be widened to at least 23ft and a separate 3ft-wide footpath laid; the tramway itself was to occupy a raised reservation on the right. There was also at this time a minor dispute with the Council over some common land on the Orme, in the care of the ecclesiastical

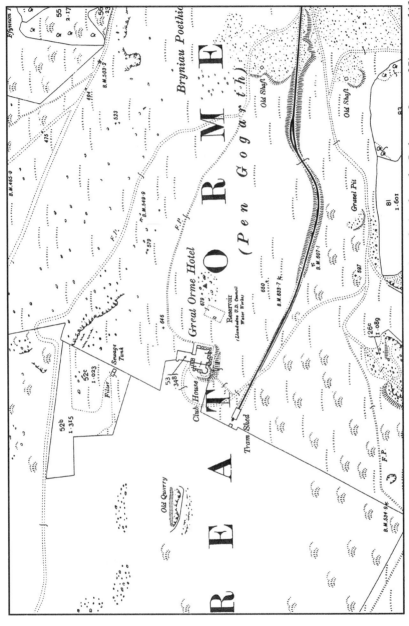

The tramway from the upper section passing loop to Summit Station, again as depicted on the Ordnance Survey 25in map of 1913. Also shown are the Great Orme Hotel, the UDC's reservoir and the actual summit point of the headland.

authorities, which had been leased to the Company for a nominal sum (£10). The Council was somewhat annoyed over this and tried to claim ownersip with the obvious intention of extracting a much higher rent but was forced to admit defeat since the claim was invalid.

On 2 August the *Chronicle* reported:

The construction of the Great Orme Tramroad is proceeding apace, and the work of laying down the rails is getting on most satisfactory. A portion of the tramroad may be expected to be in working order in about three weeks.

The report was optimistic for the steel cables, made out of 'Langlay' pattern plough steel by the St Helens Cable Co Ltd, were not in fact delivered until early May 1902 when each was hauled up to the winding house by a team of twelve horses; the winding house was sited where the two sections of the tramway met as the empowering Act – at the insistence of Lord Mostyn – forbade its erection in the town. (The boilers for the steam-driven plant had previously been hauled up by a traction engine fitted with a winch; the traction engine had moved forward a short distance and then winched the boiler up to it before moving forward again. The process had then been repeated for the second boiler.) On Friday 23 May one cable was laid in the conduit which housed it on the paved lower section, and linked to a car at the lower terminus. The car was then wound up to Halfway Station, let down and wound up again, apparently to the satisfaction of all concerned for exactly one week later the second cable was run out and attached to its car. The lower section was now ready for thorough testing before its mandatory Board of Trade inspection. Events were slightly behind schedule still, for at the half-yearly meeting of the directors on 28 February 1902 it had been announced that the line would be opened sometime in May and that – with lofty ambition – the Prince of Wales himself, who was scheduled to be touring the vicinity at the time, had been asked to perform the opening ceremony! (In the event the Prince – by now the as yet uncrowned King Edward VII – was occupied by far more pressing matters such as recuperation after a dangerous operation and his forthcoming coronation.

Meanwhile the GOT Co was busy searching for a General Manager for the tramway and in May offered the post to a Mr A. Paton, an engineer and North Wales agent for the Liverpool & North Wales Steamship Co Ltd. He declined the offer. At the same time the Company informed the Council that it would not place advertisements on the carriage windows but would confine them to the interior woodwork. In mid-July the Council gave the Company permission, on payment of 1s (5p) per annum, to attach eight small signs to lampposts and erect a larger board on a grass plot in the town's North Parade, in order to direct visitors to the lower terminus. The Company had by now been successful in its search for a manager, George White having been 'poached' from the Liverpool Overhead Railway. The first Secretary to the Company was a local house agent, Alfred G. Pugh, who had been appointed with an office in Llewelyn Avenue.

Chapter Three
OPEN - AND SHUT

INSPECTIONS AND OPENINGS

On Wednesday 30 July 1902 the tramway was visited by Colonel von Donop, representing the Board of Trade, who, according to the *Chronicle* of 9 August,

> *made a careful inspection of the work accomplished. He put the system, known as the tail-rope, to a severe test, letting the cars down rapidly and putting on the brakes quickly, and in many ways testing the soundness of the system and its working. He expressed himself generally satisfied, and intimated that everything was efficient with the exception of one or two minor details.*

Although Sir George Newnes, the publishing magnate and promoter of the Matlock cable tramway and the Lynton & Lynmouth cliff railway (amongst other lines), had been their second choice, after the Prince of Wales, to open the tramway, the directors of the GOT Co decided that any revenue lost whilst this was organised was too important to be wasted. The lower section of the line therefore opened without delay on Thursday 31 July, the day following von Donop's visit. Hurried arrangements were made in the morning and, as the first car moved out of the lower terminus in the afternoon, the cheers of the onlookers mingled with the strain of 'God Save the King' from the assembled instruments of the Town Band. When the line closed a few hours later 439 passengers had been carried.

Since the weekend following the opening was that of the August Bank Holiday, the tramway was all set for a favourable start to life and, thanks to some excellent weather for most of the week, this was achieved. During the holiday weekend over 5,000 passengers were carried – including some 3,000 on the Monday alone. *The Chronicle* of 9 August remarked that it was *a sufficient number to indicate that a great success is awaiting this enterprising venture when it is complete. The difficulty on Monday was that the tram did not run frequently enough and kept people waiting at the stations, but this will surely be altered when the line gets into complete working order. Many persons went up the Orme on the tramway, who had never before been on it, although they had stayed in Llandudno for years.*

The cars departed at 15-minute intervals – hence they 'kept people waiting at the stations' – and by the end of the first complete week of operation nearly 12,000 single passenger journeys had been made. By 8 October, the virtual end of the holiday season, this figure had reportedly risen to 70,000. At the end of the calendar year the line closed for overhaul, having carried 75,738 passengers and collected a total revenue of £925 3s 10d (£925.19) of which no less than £922 17s 3d (£922.86) came from passenger receipts. Against this was set an expenditure of £527 13s 3d (£527.66) and the sum of £397 10s 7d ((£397.53) was forwarded to the next half-year's accounts. These figures were reported with evident satisfaction at the GOT Co's half-yearly meeting on 6 March 1903. Mr J.L. Mayger and Mr T. Esmor Hooson (who had joined the board since the incorporation of the Company) were re-elected as directors.

It was hoped to reopen the lower section of the tramway (it had closed after services finished on Saturday 3 January) at Easter after the work of overhauling, repairing and checking the line had been carried out; it was reported that this work was progressing satisfactorily. As regards the upper section though, the outlook was not quite so bright. To oversee the construction work Gowrie Colquhoun Aitchison, Secretary and General Manager of the Snowdon Mountain Tramroad and described in the *Chronicle* of 14 March 1903 as 'an expert in mountain railways', was appointed as a consulting engineer. The result was, according to the same report, that 'the work on the upper portion of the tramway is progressing satisfactorily under his supervision'. The Chairman of the board reported that 'owing to unforeseen difficulties the upper section of the tramroad had not yet been inspected by the Board of Trade, but arrangements were in hand for opening the line to the summit as early as possible'. Conway also reported with satisfaction that during the last half-year another 514 shares had been allotted and a further allotment would take place early that month.

The date originally planned for the opening of the upper section was Whitsun but, while the lower section opened as intended on Easter Monday, this was not to be. The newly-completed portion was inspected - again by Colonel von Donop - on 8 May; the following extract from the *Chronicle* of 30 May describes the event:

> *Colonel von Donop, on behalf of the Board of Trade, recently inspected the upper section of the Great Orme's Head Tramroad, and, subject to certain minor alterations, the Board of Trade have passed the line and the cars for traffic. As soon as the changes required, which are cheifly connected with the brakes to the cars, have been carried out the railway will be worked to the summit. In the meantime the cars are running every quarter of an hour on the lower section up to the plateau.*

After the necessary modifications had been made the upper portion was inspected again on 7 July and passed for traffic. The opening took place the next morning, a Wednesday, without ceremony. The Great Orme Tramway was at last fully operational.

DEVELOPMENTS, DISPUTES - AND DANGER

For three years the GOT Co was embroiled in a flurry of activity which then abruptly died down, leaving the tramway to operate without major incident for a long period. The main, physical developments centred on the two ends of the tramway: at the lower a new station was planned and at the upper a hotel and golf course. Early in 1903 Llandudno UDC had approached the Company with regard to the state of the footpath in front of the station in Church Walks; the Company replied that it was willing to 'curb and channel' the path when the site had been developed in the near future. As the footpath had in fact never been kerbed or guttered before, this answer was accepted.

The number of passengers carried in 1903 was 77,410 – slightly down on the previous year. To the profit earned was added another

£1,000 from an increased share issue to pay for the construction of the new lower terminus. This task occupied the winter of 1903-04 and involved demolishing the Victoria Hotel building and removing the sharply-curved track into the old hotel yard terminus, the line now carrying straight on parallel with Old Road to almost the edge of Church Walks. (The Victoria Hotel had been one of the first to be constructed in Llandudno and was for a long time the principal hotel in the town.) At the same time three stone car sheds were erected: one at the upper end of the lower section and one at each end of the upper section. Each shed was just large enough to hold one car (with an inspection pit beneath the rails for maintenance purposes), the fourth passenger car being housed in the roofed platform area – complete with inspection pit – by the new lower terminal building at 62 Church Walks; known as Victoria Station, this became the home of the Company's registered office.

The reason for building the car sheds (and Victoria Station) was a simple one: protection of the tramcars - the car left at Summit was especially susceptible to being blown over during the winter! (The most recent occurrence of such an event is thought to have been on 27 September 1982, the car in question being No 7. A bus service was substituted until the tramway reopened a few days later.)

Meanwhile work was progressing at the summit on the development of the whole of the area. The 1898 Act empowered the Company to build an hotel there but, as it had found difficulty in even raising sufficient capital to build the tramway, it offered the chance of constructing the hotel elsewhere. The *Chronicle* of 7 February 1903 announced that Griffith B. Morgan, the catering manager of the Great Northern Railway of Ireland and owner of the Clarence Hotel in Llandudno, had recently purchased the 'Old Telegraph Inn' at the summit and proposed to spend £2,000 on extending the building to make it suitable for the increased business the tramway was expected to bring. Three weeks later Morgan was advertising for tenders for the construction of refreshment rooms adjacent to the Telegraph Inn. By the end of May the old buildings had been almost completely demolished and permission granted to Morgan to erect a marquee for the summer trade, presumably a temporary measure while the new hotel was completed. On 4 September that year the first ascent of the Great Orme by a motor car was made.

The contract for building the new hotel had been awarded to Thomas McDonald, of Dundalk, who had begun work in April 1903; by 1904 however, with the hotel only half completed, Morgan (who had by now been made a GOT Co director) went bankrupt and the sprawling, mainly one-storey structure was taken over by the Liverpool Docks Trustees who ran it as a luxury hotel (whilst continuing to track ships bound for the Mersey). Morgan's other interest at the summit, a 175-acre 18-hole golf course on land leased from Lord Mostyn, was acquired by local golfers who formed the Great Orme Golf Club for the purpose.

One other major alteration to take place during this period concerned the crossing of Tŷ Gwyn Road by the tramway. As originally laid, the crossing was widely regarded as unsafe and gave the Council especially much cause for concern. As early as September 1902 the Company had agreed to pay the UDC the sum of £17 10s (£17.50) towards the cost of putting Tŷ Gwyn Road in repair; there was also a dispute over the residents' footpath from Black Gate up the road. (The matter appears to have rested there until November 1903 when the Council informed the Company that unless the unsafe condition of the road was rectified the Board of Trade would have to be informed. In March the following year the town surveyor met the tramway directors to discuss the situation and the Company agreed, after the coming season, to take up all the track there and relay it on a more southerly site (which would mean it crossed Tŷ Gwyn Road at more of a right angle). The Company also undertook to take up the existing setts – the paving blocks between and beside the rails – and relay them and the rails more carefully, to provide wooden in lieu of iron covers for the pulley pits, and to make the gate open further back. Thus can be deduced the essential points of disagreement! This arrangement was to the satisfaction of the Council, though complaints were naturally still made throughout the year. In August the Council requested that the Company place a man at the crossing while the trams were running, until the end of the season, because of the continuing danger but it is not known whether this action was actually carried out. The matter did not end there for the start of the work on the track alteration was continually held up by lack of money. The proposed new layout was not inspected (on site) by von Donop until 19 June 1906; he approved the plans and the work was at last executed the following winter, bringing the total outlay on the tramway to £19,464.

The tramway may have seemed in fine (and much-improved) shape in outward appearance, but underneath the surface a host of disputes had been brewing during the construction period. It would be tedious to mention all in detail, and the building of the tramway was probably no different from any other civil engineering project of its time with engineers and contractors squabbling over any number of things - in this instance chiefly the type of rails, the condition of the track and cables, and the design of the rolling stock! The following example will suffice to give a flavour of the time. The plaintiffs, Messrs Thomas & John Owen, issued a writ for £80 19s 2d (£80.96) which they claimed was owing to them from the defendants, R. White & Sons, for work completed by 1 August 1901, the outstanding balance of which had not been paid. The defendants had promised to do this on receipt of a certificate for the work from their engineer Taylor, but this had not been forthcoming. The plaintiffs denied that their work had been in any way defective and instigated legal proceedings. The case was heard at Chester County Court at the end of July 1903, before Sir Horatio Lloyd, and adjourned until November. Whites then claimed that £500 had been paid in respect of a total bill of £580 19s 2d (£580.96) but the work in dispute, a concrete conduit, had not been completed and they had had to finish it themselves. The case was then further adjourned until the following March when, after three days of investigations and decision making, the judge awarded the Owens damages amounting to £67 12s (£67.60).

There then followed a long, apparently uneventful era of operations, though during the 1900s several seasons were far from satisfactory financially - sometimes the line only worked a six-week season. On the positive side, Llandudno was now growing apace - a development not unconnected with the fact that Mostyn

Estates were now granting building leases of 999 years rather than the original period of 99 years. A number of apparently trivial events though took place which, with the benefit of hindsight, can now be seen to have been of ominous significance. In 1904 George White was dismissed as Manager, apparently for expressing misgivings concerning the operation of the tramway. White thereupon wrote to the Board of Trade, claiming that the emergency brake on the (lower section) cars was defective, the slipper brakes on the upper section cars had been removed, and that an accident due to overwinding the cars had not been reported. When contacted by the Board of Trade, the Company insisted that the emergency brakes were satisfactory and that the slipper brakes had in fact been removed by White himself without permission, but made no comment about the alleged accident (which had occurred on 8 October 1902 when the top car on the upper section had been pulled up rather than down). It was in fact the first in a series of such mishaps and when White's successor, Henry Sutcliffe, was appointed in 1906 he promptly removed the emergency brakes – and the related overspeed governor on the winding engine. It was to prove a terrible decision in every sense of the word.

Other events of note during this period were: in 1909 the Council was given the chance to purchase the tramway but its offered price of £7,000 was deemed to low by the shareholders (though not the directors); in 1909 and 1911 two minor collisions occurred, but without serious damage or injury; during World War I the Summit Hotel was occupied by service personnel; in 1918 the tramway only operated a total of twenty-two days as a new cable was needed and a permit for one could not be obtained from the Ministry of Munitions because of the war effort, and in 1924 a booking office and shop were added to Victoria Station. Underneath this apparent calm, though, several disturbing factors were quietly at work, awaiting only for the opportunity and right circumstances to align themselves in a disasterous - and tragic - combination.

MISFORTUNE STRIKES

On Sunday 21 August 1932 the drawbar of one of the lower section cars (No 5) snapped in two, though luckily the car had been brought to a halt without any mishap. Just two days later the same thing happened again, this time though with far more terrible consequences:

> *All Llandudno was horrified on Tuesday to learn that one of the cable cars of the Great Orme tramway had run away, crushing to death the driver, Edward Harris, and creating some shocking injuries among the crowd of visitors who, a moment before, had been gaily singing as they returned from a happy morning on the summit of the Orme. A little girl, Margaret Worthington, whose foot was torn off, died at 3pm in the hospital.*
>
> (*North Wales Chronicle* 26 August 1932)

The runaway occurred shortly after noon in Tŷ Gwyn Road, just above Black Gate. As the *Chronicle* continued:

> *Careering for a short distance at gathering speed, the tram left the metals and crashed into a twelve foot high wall. A tramway standard caught in its flight was torn up, a portion being flung into a neighbouring lane. As the top of the tram swept along the crest of the wall, it dislodged the coping stones which cascaded through the window spaces upon the passengers. The car was full of people, there probably being thirty-five people on it.*

At the moment of collision the car's occupants were hurled violently forward, many breaking their heads on the window frames. The wall in question was that on the left (looking downhill) at the top of the narrow Old Road. The unfortunate brakeman on the front platform tried to jump to safety but tragically chose the wrong side for the car lurched over, crushing him against the wall. Riding on the platform with him was 12-year-old Margaret Worthington who had been to take her father, an employee of the tramway company, his lunch at the summit. Harris had courageously grabbed the young girl and leapt from the tram with her in his arms; there she was found, alive but badly injured, pinned by the weight of the tramcar against the wall. She could not be freed until help arrived to move the car but by then it was too late; she died three hours later in hospital. The conductor, Jim Coleburn, who had been riding on the rear platform, had also jumped but had escaped uninjured.

The scene was one of utter chaos with crowds of onlookers beseiging the rescue workers – many of whom were themselves injured passengers – and a constant ambulance shuttle service taking the casualties to hospital. In all two died, eleven were kept in hospital for treatment and three others treated there for cuts and shock. One of those badly injured was the wife of a Manchester rabbi – who escaped unscathed himself, as did the Bishop of Killaloe, another passenger. With the injured removed the area was roped-off and the car, No 4, secured by ropes to a pair of convenient trees to await the Ministry of Transport investigation.

The inquiry, held by Lt Col E.P. Anderson, took place the following Monday in Llandudno Town Hall. It lasted one hour, the scene of the accident having been previously inspected by Anderson. In the words of the *Chronicle* of 2 September, 'Several facts of interest were disclosed during the course of the inquiry'. One was when the Manager, Sutcliffe, recounted how a drawbar had broken the Sunday before the accident. It had been, he said, a unique occurrence. All the drawbars were identical, made of 'Vibrac' steel, and had been supplied by Craven Bros Ltd of Manchester. A representative of this company said that the drawbars were capable of taking a direct strain of 300-400 tons; he was of the opinion that 'the break had occurred sideways and was not in the direction of the tension'. Sutcliffe stated that the Company – the GOT Co – 'did not specify any particular strength or analysis. The makers knew the conditions. There was no specifications with the drawbars previously supplied'.

At Anderson's insistence the broken drawbar – which had connected the tramcar to the cable - was produced by the police. It had been manufactured to a uniform thickness of $3/_4$in to enable it to run in the conduit slot, which was $1^1/_4$in wide, thus allowing room for clearance. On being measured it was discovered that the drawbar had been worn down $1/_8$in in thickness – by what Sutcliffe termed 'surface rubbing' – since its fitting *on 15 August*. The next intriguing piece of information was remarkable by its absence: though the car's wheel and slipper brakes (see Chapter Seven for details) were both found to be hard on, they had failed to halt the runaway progress of the car – 24ft along the rails after parting company with the cable and a further 75ft down the roadway. Of the car's emergency slot brake, which should have automatically come into play immediately the drawbar broke, and would have been sufficient to stop the car, *there was no mention*. The rest of the investigation was conducted in private. (Author's italics.)

The mystery of the missing emergency brake was cleared up by the publication of the inspecting officer's report on 2 February 1933. It transpired that during the period 1902-06 jerky handling of the winding controls had caused momentary slackness in the cable sufficient to cause the automatic brake to come into play. This brake comprised two jaws bearing on the Z-shaped sides of the conduit slot; the normal tension on the cable held them off. If however the tension was removed, ie by the cable breaking or suddenly slackening, powerful springs forced the jaws against the sides of the conduit. Moreover, the weight of the car continuing downhill was transmitted by means of cams to the jaws, causing them to bear with increasing pressure until the car was brought to a halt. It was an apparently foolproof and very effective emergency brake; however, the constant interruptions to services in the tramway's early years – it took several hours' work to release and reset the brake - had resulted in the removal of the brake apparatus (and the overspeed governor on the winding engine). More importantly though, these actions had apparently been taken without the knowledge, let alone approval, of the board of directors.

Anderson did not have to look far for the cause of the accident. Besides the disconnection of the emergency brake, he also condemmed the use of steel treated in a way unsuitable for the purpose intended on the tramway, ie the drawbars. He recommended strongly that all similar drawbars should be replaced, and that passengers should be prohibited from riding on the front platforms of the cars. Above all, he emphasised the necessity of complying with statutory regulations. Operations had of course been suspended ever since the accident, pending the publication of the report.

On Monday 13 February the GOT Co held its annual general meeting at which an advisory committee was set up, made up of three directors and three shareholders, to implement the advice of Anderson's report. Action had already been taken in one direction, for the directors had consulted the Liverpool firm of Messrs Sloan & Lloyd Barnes over the question of a new, trouble-free design of emergency brake, the details of which were now with the Ministry of Transport for approval. Receipts for 1932 were given as £3,446 10s 11d (£3,446.55), the overall result being a loss of £91 15s 2d (£91.76) attributable to the suspension of services and the sum of £150 expended on repairing car No 4 and the track. The hope was expressed of reopening the line in time for Easter. Mention was made of the fact that in the previous 30 years over 4 million passengers had been carried without a single accident; indeed, the meeting dwelt upon past success rather than present uncertainty. And there was great uncertainty, for the directors reluctantly admitted that the Company possessed no reserve fund and that the claims for compensation (still being finalised) were not fully covered by insurance. (In the light of what had emerged about the running of the tramway, the Company's insurers had, not unnaturally, repudiated liability.)

The logical outcome of this state of affairs was obvious – and inevitable:

Surprise was caused in Llandudno yesterday when it became known that a Sheriff's Officer had under a writ of fi. fa., taken possession of the Great Orme Tramway Co. The first intimation of this unexpected development that the townspeople had was the appearance of bills announcing that the county bailiff, Mr. W. Owen, F.I.A., of Llandudno, would "sell by public auction at the Victoria Station, Church Walks, on Monday, June 12th, the whole of the fixtures, fittings, and office equipment, relating to the Great Orme Tramway Company, and including 4½ miles of trams rails, approximately 870

yards of steel cable, and four tram cars (48 seats)."
                                    (North Wales Weekly News 8 June 1933)

This action came three weeks after a suit for damages, filed by Rabbi H. Levin and his wife Sarah of Cheetham Hill, Manchester for £4,000 in respect of injuries and shock received in the accident, was settled for £1,000 plus costs. Thus the directors failed in their attempt to persuade those claiming against the tramway to wait until the line was working again and earning revenue out of which they could be paid. The Company's financial position can best be judged by the fact that it was unable to meet even Levin's reduced damages and therefore applied for and obtained a write of *fi. fa.* (a sheriff's order to sell the goods of a debtor in execution of a judgement).

An emergency meeting of the GOT Co was held on 7 June under the chairmanship of Alderman John Owen, the outcome being that the directors had little choice in the circumstances but to file a petition in the High Court for a compulsory winding-up order. Mr R. Vincent Johnson, director and solicitor for the GOT Co, spoke of being fair to the other creditors. (Other claims lodged against the Company amounted to a further £10,000.) He stated that there was 'no reason why the trams should not be operated after the liquidation, because an asset to the town as valuable as this could not be allowed to disappear'. They were prophetic words.

Chapter Four
NEW OWNERS

THE GREAT ORME RAILWAY LTD

Matters were meanwhile well in hand to have the tramway running again. A new set of emergency brakes had been ordered from Walker Bros of Pagefield Ironworks, Wigan and one had been fitted to car No 5 and tested in April 1933. Testing continued throughout the summer, while the winding-up petition was adjourned for a month to see if some agreement could be reached with the Company's creditors. No such understanding was forthcoming though and on Monday 24 July, in the Chancery Division of the High Court, Mr Justice Bennett made an order for the compulsory liquidation of the Great Orme Tramway Company. (The Winding-up Order had been applied for by the Company on 7 June, and was not opposed.) A liquidator was appointed on 4 September, with control of assets amounting to the value of £6,839 3s 0d (£6,839.15).

A creditors' meeting was held on 25 August and it was decided that the best course of action was to continue the brake tests with a view to reopening the line and then selling it as a going – and proven safe – concern. A public test of the new brake on car No 5, laden with scrap iron, was held on 23 March 1934 before film cameras. The trial was a success and Walker Bros subsequently equipped No 4 in similar fashion. Successful too was the Ministry of Transport's inspection (by Colonel A.C. Trench) on 11 May that year and less than a week later, on Thursday 17 May, the tramway reopened for business. (A new regulation imposed as a consequence of the 1932 accident was a compulsory brake test each spring before the seasonal opening.) Also successful was the period of operation that summer and the line was accordingly offered for sale by the liquidator.

In December 1934 the tramway was sold for £5,600 to a syndicate which originated from the shareholders' committee, and the new owners set about forming a limited company to operate the line the following year. Thus, on 25 March 1935, the Great Orme

Railway Ltd was registered with a capital of £10,000 in £10 shares. The six directors were John E. Anstiss (draper), Hugh Edwards (painter), Chairman Arthur Hewitt (architect), Sir William M. Letts, John E. Payne (café proprietor) and Arthur Sutcliffe (described as a gentleman); all were local men. The ownership of the tramway was transferred on 30 March.

The line opened for the 1935 summer season for business as usual, and settled down to its previous pattern of seasonal operation for the rest of the decade. Operation was not suspended during World War II, though the Orme was commandeered by the Army and the Summit Hotel converted into an RAF radar station; it is believed the trams continued to run, if only intermittently – possibly as cover for the activities going on in the vicinity. (A very similar situation existed with regard to the nearby Snowdon Mountain Railway and its Summit Hotel.)

The war had changed people's social habits forever – especially with regard to their leisure and holiday activities. Edwardian-style relaxation was no longer in vogue, however sumptuous the premises, and after the RAF moved out the 29-bedroom hotel was reborn as the 'Great Orme International Sporting and Holiday Centre' before being put up for auction in 1949; the whole complex failed to sell, though the golf course was later purchased separately by Howell Jones, a local farmer and town councillor, and returned to grazing land. In 1952 the hotel – by now reduced to the life of a summer-only café with much of the structure left empty – was again offered for sale. This time it was bought for £10,000 – by a partnership headed by Randolph Turpin, the boxer, for resurrection as a sporting complex. This venture failed too and in 1961 Turpin was declared bankrupt. The building was then acquired by the Council and subsequently leased to a succession of owners and is now a vibrant leisure complex of shops, restaurant and bar.

Apart from slight changes in identification necessitated by the tramway's new name, and several service changes (see later), the only major event which happened during the tramway's period of new ownership was when, at the end of the 1945 season, Henry Sutcliffe – Manager since 1906 – was succeeded by Mr C.C. Rhodes.

His retirement in effect marked the end of the old order for just two years later Llandudno UDC decided to buy the tramway.

UNDER CIVIC OWNERSHIP

Under the provisions of the 1898 authorising Act, Llandudno Urban District Council had been given the option of purchasing the tramway after a period of 28 years had elapsed (ie in 1926) or at seven-yearly intervals thereafter. When one such opportunity came round in 1947 the Council took the decision to exercise this option and served the necessary notice on the GOR Ltd. The Company calculated that the price the Council would have to pay would be £26,000 – a figure based on the capital expended since 1898 (£19,464) plus interest. The Council took exception to this unrealistic figure in view of the fact that the line had been purchased in 1935 for only £5,600 to which could be added further capital expenditure of just £1,370! The Council was supported in its view by Mr Justice Jenkins in the Chancery Division of the High Court when he ruled that the purchase price was to be based on outlay since 1935 only which, plus interest, gave a compulsory purchase price of £8,407. Payment was made by the Council on 24 November 1948, back-dated to 31 March, and civic ownership took effect from New Year's Day following. The GOR Ltd was then left with little else to do but wind itself up voluntarily, with its last meeting held on 25 March 1950. The final settlement to shareholders amounted to 33s 9d (£1.69) per £1 share.

After some track relaying had been carried out on the lower section, the tramway opened again at Easter as usual and continued to prosper, though in the following year (1951) the Council introduced competition for the line in the shape of a bus service from the Town Hall to St Tudno's church. (This service also ran in the winter months as far as Ty'n y Coed Road and proved a boon to residents living on the Orme.) Further track renewal was later carried out, made possible by good returns from the line (some $1/4$ million passengers were being carried annually), but by the mid-1950s it was clear that costs were rising far too rapidly and some method of reducing them would have to be found. One obvious area in which economies could be made was that of power: the boiler house at Halfway burnt some 250 tons of coke each year at a cost of £7 per ton. It was estimated that if the winding house was converted to electricity then approximately £1,400 could be saved each year; thus in 1956 a contract was placed with the English Electric Co Ltd for the necessary plant and the steam winding engines were used for the last time during the 1957 season. By the time the tramway reopened in 1958 the conversion had been carried out.

During the next three decades little change was made to either the tramway or its methods of working, though in 1965 a brick passenger shelter was erected at the Summit Station – prospective passengers caught in the rain there could at long last keep dry. At the begining of August 1966 a slight mishap occurred on the upper section when the rear bogie of a Summit-bound car took the wrong line at the passing loop, causing the two cars to collide. No-one was hurt in the incident but the tramway was out of action for several days while the damage was repaired. In 1968 Mr Rhodes, the General Manager, retired at the end of the season and was succeeded by Eric Woodyatt, the Manager of the UDC motor buses, who took a new position of Transport Manager covering both systems. In the following year a second rival to the line appeared on the scene in the form of the privately-owned Great Orme Cabinlift. Using 42 closed, 4-seater cabins on a 10,750ft-long continuous steel cable supported on nine pylons, this runs in a straight line, roughly parallel to the GOT on its northern side, from Camera Hill overlooking Happy Valley to a point just east of the Summit Hotel. Whilst the ride up or down the Orme (9 minutes in either direction) was considerably quicker than that offered by the GOT, the fare charged was considerably more and the lift was consequently not regarded as a threat to the tramway.

On Monday 30 July 1972 the 70th anniversary of the tramway was celebrated (albeit one day early) with cheering crowds, Edwardian costumes worn by performers from the Arcadia Theatre and the Pier Pavilion, and the 11.00am car conducted by the Chairman of the Council, Harold Gott. Also present was Mr E.

Johnson, representative of Messrs R. White & Sons, suppliers of the original track and winding gear. Every passenger that day was presented with a special commemorative certificate to mark the occasion; special one-day postal covers were also sold – and promptly sold-out. Some 1,600 passengers were carried, though the squally weather of the day led Eric Woodyatt to remark that "It is a good job we had a celebration otherwise we would have had a poor day for revenue"!

In 1973 the line joined, for marketing purposes, the growing ranks of the 'Great Little Trains of Wales', a fitting way to honour the principality's last surviving tramway. A year later, as from 1 April 1974 following the nation-wide reorganisation of local government, the tramway came under the control of the Tourism & Amentities Department of Aberconwy Borough Council,which body absorbed the former Llandudno UDC.

Although passenger figures fell slightly in 1976 compared with 1975 (191,490 and 208,000 respectively), the high standard of maintenance undertaken augured well for the tramway's long-term survival under the new Council. In 1976 for example, a new type of oil-impregnated nylon bush was tested on a cable pulley on the lower section, with satisfactory results, and a further twenty-five were ordered for the 1977 season as the first stage of a general replacement programme. (The advantages of this type of bush are that they need no lubrication, less inspection and are easily replaced. A boon to local lineside residents is that they are also quieter!)

The 75th anniversary of the line – now officially titled the Great Orme Tramway once again - was celebrated over the weekend of 30/31 July 1977. The scenes were much as for the 70th anniversary with decorated cars, travellers in period costume and so forth. On the Sunday over 2,000 people were carried and at Victoria Station the Mayor of Aberconwy, Councillor K. David Jones, unveiled a plaque commemorating the tramway's history. During the winter of 1977/78 some £38,000 was spent on repairs to the track on the lower section, though this meant that the line did not operate an Easter service in 1978 – the first time it had failed to do so for a great many years.

The tradition of celebrating milestones in the tramway's life was maintained when, on 31 July 1982, the 80th anniversary of its opening was marked by visits from the Mayor and the Town Band. Passenger journeys that year totalled 120,581 with the figure continuing the gradual downwards trend evident since the mid-1970s. By the middle of the decade it had dropped to close to the 100,000 mark and, with the tramway running at a loss for several years, in 1987 the Council advertised it for sale or lease. It seemed that after spending half its life under municipal control, the Great Orme Tramway was about to 'go private' once again.

Chapter Five
THE FUNICULAR SYSTEM

This is perhaps an appropriate point at which to pause in the recounting of the chronological account of the Great Orme Tramway and, instead, focus upon exactly what makes it unique in the British Isles. The specialised function of much of its equipment – the purely mechanical side of the tramway – deserves closer inspection than has been given it so far, and this facet of the line is now dealt with in the following three sections: the permanent way, the winding gear, and the communication system.

THE PERMANENT WAY

The rails used on both 3ft 6in gauge sections are of the flat-bottom, railway type, and weigh 50lb per yard. The original rails were manufactured in Workington and supplied by White & Sons, together with points and crossings manufactured in Sheffield by Askham Bro & Wilson Ltd. On the upper section the rails are bolted in 30ft lengths to wooden sleepers, lightly ballasted, laid on the ground in railway fashion. On the lower section, an entirely different arrangement was called for. Here the rails are bolted to short sleepers laid in a bed of concrete, and connected by ties at 6ft intervals to two parallel Z-section girders laid back to back down the centre of the track. The girders form a 6in-wide conduit, 14in deep with a $1^{1}/_{4}$in gap between the girder flanges at the top; the haulage cable runs within this conduit. The running rails are fitted with continuous guard rails – a specification of the Board of Trade for the GOT Co had intended to use grooved tramway rails – made of 23lb per yard angle irons. The whole is paved flush with the rail and conduit surfaces, this being done on the roadway stretch with tarmac and, on the reserved roadside stretch up to Halfway, with concrete.

On the tramway's lower section the cable runs, in its conduit, supported on grooved sheaves and guided round curves by vertical pulleys spaced at 6ft intervals. The pulleys are mounted in a special housing with an access cover in the roadway for lubrication and other maintenance purposes. On the upper section, the cable runs exposed (except at short road crossings) on similar sheaves and pulleys.

At the upper section passing loop the two points in the track are worked by the passage of the cars, with each car setting the points as it trails through the switch blades in readiness for its return along the same path. Hand-levers are also fitted but these are locked inside wire cages to prevent any possible tampering. On top of each lever (one each side of the running line) is a circular indicator bearing a number corresponding to the car using that side of the loop – the fact that each car sets the points behind it when it leaves the loop means that it always takes the same track through the loop (ie the north or south track), as indeed it must do to prevent the haulage cables from crossing. Guarded breaks in the running rails allow for the free passage of the cable. It is unusual with this type of funicular operation to have worked switches with moving blades; on such lines abroad, particularly in Switzerland, points have fixed rails with appropriate gaps and the cars have double-flanged wheels on one side and flangeless wheels on the other – the two cars have their flanged wheels on opposite sides to guide them consistently through their 'own' side of the loop. Double-flanged wheels could not be used however with the flush road surfaces of the Great Orme line, hence the existing point design.

A similarly – worked set of points controls entry to, and exit from, the lower end of the loop on the lower section with a wide junction slot where the conduit divides. (At night and during the winter this gap is protected by a metal cover.) At the upper end of the loop the two tracks only converge precisely far enough to become – just within the definition – interlaced, the two nearest rails running together to form a common running rail/guard rail unit. This arrangement provides a 'single line' while at the same time allows two separate conduits to be used, each in the centre of their own track, so that the ascending and descending cables do not meet on the sharp curves and therefore foul the pulleys, as would happen if a single conduit were used. (This problem is avoided on the upper section of the tramway by the fact that off-centre drawbars are used on the cars, enabling the separate cables to run between one pair of rails with sufficient distance between them to prevent fouling.)

All pulleys and sheaves are kept lubricated throughout the course of every operating day, and indeed the whole of the permanent way checked, by two maintenance men employed specifically for this purpose.

THE WINDING GEAR

As installed for the opening of the line, this was a steam-powered plant comprising one boiler and two colliery-type winding engines (as used for raising and lowering pit cages). The locomotive-type boiler – with a second, smaller one in reserve – was built by Robey & Co Ltd of Lincoln and supplied steam at just over 100lbs per square inch pressure to the two engines, one for each section. Both the latter were supplied by C. & A. Musker of Liverpool, that working the lower section having 12in bore and 14in stroke cylinders and an output of 80hp whilst that of the upper, less steep section, had 8in x 12in cylinders and an output of 60hp. It would appear that these were soon discovered to be not quite up to their allotted tasks and during the winter of 1913/14 the larger engine was moved to replace the smaller one and a new, 120hp engine was purchased from the Sandicroft Foundry, Chester, to work the lower section. All three engines were of a two-cylinder design and were governor-controlled to a constant speed – at least, they were originally but, as it emerged at the 1932 investigation, the governors were removed early in the tramway's life. Each of the pair in use drove a shaft fitted with two 5ft 4in – diameter winding drums, one wound the opposite way to the other so that when the shaft turned one drum would wind cable in and the other let it out, and vice versa, thus working the two cars in opposite directions on each section of the tramway.

Water for the boilers was obtained from the Council reservoir, completed in 1901, on top of the Orme; water was pumped up to this to supply the buildings on the headland and, in return for a

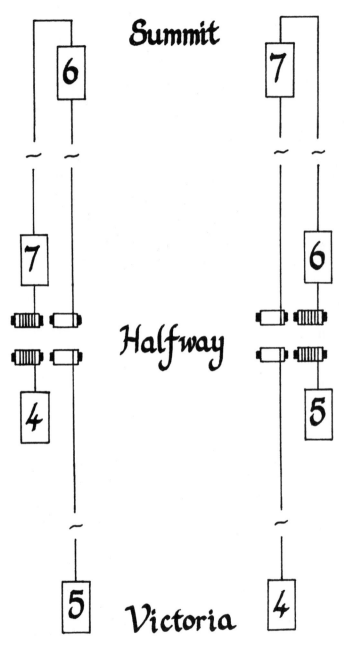

Summit

Halfway

Victoria

Schematic winding diagram for the tramway showing, left and right, the two extremes of travel of cars and cables.

financial consideration, a feeder main was connected from it to the engine house. At the end of the 1920s a new, purpose-built boiler house was erected by the winding house and both the original boilers replaced by a single, larger secondhand one.

By the mid-1950s it was clear that the whole power plant was nearing the end of its working life; indeed for successive seasons the boiler's working pressure had had to be reduced for safety reasons and it would shortly have become useless. Drastic action was obviously called for and the decision was taken to change over to electric winding, primarily on the grounds of cost-efficiency. Accordingly, during the winter of 1957/58 the original plant was removed and replaced by completely new gear installed by the English Electric Co Ltd; this company also supplied the new electrical equipment whilst the new mechanical gear was designed and built by John Mills & Co (Llanidloes) Ltd. Each drum shaft is now driven by a 50Hz 3-phase slip-ring induction motor, supplied with electricity at 415V; the motor working the lower section shaft is rated at 125hp and that of the upper at 75hp. Both run at 730rpm and are geared down to give drum speeds of 25rpm and 35rpm for the lower and upper sections respectively. To ensure smooth starting and stopping drum controllers, operating rotor resistances, controls the motor speeds. These dual controls are mounted on a common control panel, together with an emergency stop switch and handbrake wheel, this last operating screw-down brakes on the winding drums. A weight-operated brake is also incorporated into the equipment and is continually held in the 'off' position whenever the current is on by an electro-hydraulic thruster; if the emergency stop button is pushed, or a centrifugal trip on one of the motors (set to cut-out at 15% overspeed) comes into action, then so does the emergency brake. The screw handbrake provides the normal means of control braking and is fully interlocked with the rest of the controls. The two sets of controls are the separate responsibility of two engineers, or winchmen, with one in charge of each section of the tramway.

A week before Easter every year, as part of the tramway's mandatory annual inspection, the winding equipment is thoroughly checked and the gear drive modified, by means of

Great Orme Tramway Centenary

Souvenir Ticket

Issued to commemorate 100 years of cable hauled heritage

27th July to 4th August 2002

In past years the GOT has never been been marketed as strenuously as it deserves. This beermat from its 'Railway' period is a rare promotional exception.

temporary belts, so as to produce a drum speed high enough to cause the cars on the lower section to bypass their pre-set brake limits and thus test their emergency conduit brakes.

As is to be expected, since the winding house is only halfway up the line of the tramway and not at the summit, different methods of moving the cars have to be employed on the two sections. On the lower section this is by using two separate steel cables, each $1^5/_{16}$in in diameter, $1/_2$ mile long and with a breaking strain of 60 tons.

Each cable is wound onto one drum and attached to one car; consequently when one car is wound up the other is lowered down, and vice versa. This is the simplest form of funicular winding and is the method used on the majority of British cliff railways.

On the upper section a different system is called for, utilising three separate cables each with a diameter of $7/_8$in and a breaking strain of 30 tons. The first cable is wound onto one drum and linked to the lower end of one car; the second is attached to the other (upper) end of that car and continues to Summit, round a large idler wheel there and back down to join the second car. The third cable runs from the other (lower) end of that car down to the other drum in the winding house. Thus, when the drum shaft is rotated in the appropriate direction, the car at Summit is pulled *down* to Halfway Station, hauling *up* the other car in the process. As the ascending car is also connected by cable to the winding house the braking of one automatially produces the same effect upon the other, regardless of which direction it is travelling. This arrangement is known as the 'tail rope' system on account of the cables linking or attached to the tail ends of the cars, and is employed on cliff railways or other funiculars when the winding engine is situated at the bottom of the line. (Reference to the accompanying diagram should help clarify matters.)

COMMUNICATIONS

As the tramway is operated as a remotely-controlled funicular railway, a system of communication between the drivers in the cars and the winchmen in the winding house is of paramount importance. The system adopted when the tramway was constructed comprised a bell and telephone link between both cars on one section and their engineer in the winding house. Hand-cranked generators in each car supplied the necessary current to operate the equipment, and communication between the winding house and the trams was effected via an overhead wire to which the cars were connected by trolley poles. This wire was carried along the route by roadside standards and supporting brackets in a similar manner to an overhead current supply for a conventional electric tramway - indeed, the Great Orme line was sometimes mistaken for exactly that though the overhead installation was much lighter than would otherwise have been the case. Both passing loops had two overhead wires to allow the cars' trolleys to pass, though the second wire was not added to the upper section loop until 1949; before that date the conductor of a descending car would have to lower his trolley from the wire whilst the other car passed. The telephone allowed the driver of a car to talk to the engineer in the winding house in charge of his section, or to the other car driver, whilst a bell push mounted under the car's roof above the driver's head enabled him to send immediate and unabiguous instructions to the winding house (as for example if an emergency stop was required) using a system of bell codes.

In 1990 this system was deemed to have reached the end of its working life and was accordingly replaced by a radio system designed by Airlink of Llandudno. This had two functions: the first was that by depressing a foot pedal, a car driver could signal to the winding house that he was ready to start (both drivers on a section having to do so at the same time in order for the winding to start) and, second, to provide a voice link between all four cars and the winding house. (A bonus, in terms of operational costs, was that the deployment of this equipment did away for the principal reason for having a conductor on each car, namely to look after the trolleypole.) The overhead wire was removed when the new system was installed, though the iron standards still stand beside the tramway today, it having been decided to save on the expense of removing them from their very solid foundations.

In 2002 the radio link was in turn superseded, this time by an inductive loop system from Doppelmayr, the Austrian funicular specialists. Signals are relayed between winchmen and drivers via cables laid beside the track and sensors mounted below the cars, with messages displayed electronically on monitors and control panels in the winding house and cars. (A similar system is in use on the hi-tech CairnGorm Funicular Railway in Scotland, opened in December 2001, and was also installed by Doppelmayr.) A track position indicator shows the winchman exactly where on his section each tramcar is, and the cables are marked to tell him when to stop the cars at their termini.

Chapter Six
MAKING THE ASCENT

A RIDE UP THE ORME

A typical journey on the Great Orme Tramway, for an observant passenger, goes somewhat in this fashion, beginning with the purchase of a ticket at the booking office window at Victoria Station. This window is set in the side of the one-storey building which forms one side of the station premises and houses the manager's office; from this building projects an overall roof to protect the 'platform' area and the one terminal track and its car inspection pit. The other three sides of the premises are open (though railed-off) with Church Walks at the lower end and Old Road to the side opposite the office block. Car No 4 or 5 is boarded when it arrives – if it is not already waiting – from ground level, there being no raised platforms in the conventional railway sense anywhere along the tramway. On leaving the terminus the car moves out into Old Road past the site of the original terminus on the left, in the former Victoria Hotel yard, 90ft above sea level.

Passing straightaway the King's Head public house – outside which on fine days an interested crowd can always be found observing the trams' comings and goings – the line climbs up the centre of the narrow thoroughfare of Old Road with its solid stone walls on either side, in the heart of what was once – as the road's name suggests – the old hamlet from which the town grew. As there is no room whatsoever for another vehicle to squeeze past, other traffic is prohibited from using the roadway during the hours of tramway operation, apart for access to the handful of houses with entrances here. It is astonishing to think that the road had to be widened before the trams could use it! The gradient over this stretch of the line fluctuates between 1 in 4.4 and 1 in 3.6 – the steepest portion being at the top of Old Road where the line enters and crosses Tŷ Gwyn Road at Black Gate. Just before this point - formerly the tramway's first request stop – was the site of the fatal 1932 crash; a large, convex mirror on one side of the line enables the driver of a descending tramcar to spot any traffic about to come round the blind corner at the road junction. Continuing up the right-hand side of Tŷ Gwyn Road, the line occupies its own unfenced and concreted reservation, slightly above the level of the road surface; this doubles as a handy pavement for those wishing to make the ascent on foot. (There is no danger of a collision with one of the slow-moving tramcars – the noise made by the cables in the conduits when the cars are in motion provides ample warning to the unwary.) Almost immediately the passing loop is reached, a little below the exact halfway mark on the section, and the descending car passed. On the right of the track along this Tŷ Gwyn Road section is the stone cliff face of Killen's Hill.

Above the passing loop the two tracks converge to form the interlaced track section described earlier, and this continues all the way up to Halfway Station. A short distance past the loop comes Ty'n y Coed Road junction on the left, formerly the site of the tramway's second and final request stop known as Ty'n y Coed Road, or Killen's Hill. When one car halted at Black Gate the other had, of necessity, to stop here – though it was not unknown for some of the more agile passengers to jump on and off a moving car with the driver only bothering to stop for the older or less infirm ones!

The line now steepens its climb and swings sharply round to the right - still paralleling the roadway – and then to the left, off the concreted reservation and away from the road which veers even more abruptly leftwards as both tramway and road enter the open heathland of the Orme's plateau. Here the ascending car comes gently to rest under the overall roof outside its stone shed, behind which stands the winding house and, beyond that, the car shed for that end of the upper section. Here passengers are invited by a large, Welsh and English language notice, to changes cars for the summit. This is the logically-named Halfway Station, originally (and equally logically) known as First Station. (Current usage favours the spelling Half Way.) At 489ft above sea level the station is exactly 400ft above the lower terminus and 872 track yards from it. (Interestingly, this figure is 90yd longer than that authorised by the 1898 Act.) The average gradient climbed in that distance is 1 in 6.5.

Originally passengers would have had to walk around the outside of the stone-built winding house and car sheds to await the arrival of car No 6 or 7 from Summit but, following the rebuilding work of the 1990s, this journey can be made along a covered walkway in what is now known as Halfway House. (See Chapter Eight.) Sadly, the rebuilding work has obliterated the final remains of one of the pair of former linking tracks between the two sections, and of the siding laid to serve the boiler house.

The upper section of the tramway commences on the flat, with an ungated level crossing on the road down to St Tudno's church a short distance out from the station, then begins to rise gently along a low embankment up to the mid-way passing loop. A little way off to the left, and well below the level of the tramway, is the entrance to the Bronze Age workings known as the Great Orme Mines, now open to the public. Though on a private right of way the track is unfenced – and, in the true British tradition of all minor lines wandering through open countryside, straying sheep and cattle are a constant hazard. (Despite Lord Mostyn's request, the GOT Co never fenced the upper section when the tramway was being constructed, and it has remained unguarded ever since.) Leaving the mid-way loop behind, the embankment gives way to a short cutting where the gradient stiffens to 1 in 10.3 – the steepest slope on the upper section - before easing abruptly as the line emerges onto the flatter area of the summit.

Summit Station, 827yd from Halfway and just out of sight from it, consisted for many years of a simple stone car shed similar to those at Halfway, outside which the car would halt. Today passengers alight under cover in the adjoining 1992 – built spacious station. (See Chapter Eight.) Again, the length of this section is at variance with that authorised by the 1898 Act, this time being nearly 71yd shorter! If, however, the distance between the Halfway termini is included – over which track was originally laid – then the discrepancy between the authorised and actual totals appears to sort itself out.

At 650ft above sea level the terminus is just 29ft below the actual summit of the Orme and 161ft above Halfway. The average gradient over the upper section is 1 in 15.5 – less than half that of the lower. On the right of the tramway as the car shed is approached is first the actual summit, then the buildings of the summit complex, whilst to the left is the fossil-rich hollow carved out of the limestone known as Bishop's Quarry, the relic of a commercial enterprise of a former Bishop of Bangor.

The view from the summit of the Great Orme is the reason for the very existence of the tramway, and it is without doubt truly impressive. From a vantage point seemingly poised midway between land and sky, the coastline extends far on each side, especially majestic in appearance to the west with its jutting headlands, the entrance to the Menai Straits and the island of Anglesey. Behind the coastal development to the south, and across the broad estuary and valley of the Conwy, rise the mountains of Snowdonia whilst to the north and east lies the Irish Sea stretching out to the horizon, broken only by the backbone of the Isle of Man and, on exceptionally clear days, by the mountains of the Lake District in England and the Wicklow Hills in Ireland.

Today the bulk of the headland is designated the Great Orme Country Park & Nature Reserve – being variously a Special Area of Conservation, a Site of Special Scientific Interest, a Heritage Coast and a Marine Special Area of Conservation – on account of the rich diversity of its wildlife: breeding colonies of kittiwakes, guillemots and razorbills on its cliffs, grey seals, dolphins and pilot whales in its coastal waters and a host of rare plant and butterfly species on its grassland. No account of the Great Orme, however, would be complete without a mention of the goats. Perhaps the most unexpected sight afforded a first-time visitor to Llandudno is that of a large, wild, Kashmir goat trotting nonchalantly up one of the town's streets. The chances are that he or she will be making its way back to the Orme, where a colony of these magnificent, long-haired creatures was established in 1890 by Lord Mostyn with animals from his own herd at Gloddeath. (The original breeding stock came from Windsor Great Park, descendants of a coronation gift from the Shah of Persia to the young Queen Victoria.) These unique residents of the Orme can often be seen perched on the rocks beside the lower section of the tramway, providing yet another spectacle for passing passengers.

OPERATION

The running of the cars on each section is controlled by the driver on each car and the section engineer, or winchman, in the winding house with communication between them effected by way of the induction loop system described earlier. On the lower section, by releasing the brake on the winding drums the engineer sets the two cars in motion at a constant speed (5mph), and by applying the screw brake he stops the cars at the end of the journey (and where needed in an emergency). The drivers on the cars do not use their own brakes during normal running – if, for example, one needs to slow for the traffic lights at Black Gate, he signals to the winchman to slow the cable accordingly.

A somewhat similar arrangement is in force on the upper section of the tramway, with the signal when ready to start being given from the lower car. Both drivers on this section however operate their handbrakes during the journey for the constant cable speed is 7mph and the more varied gradients on this section necessitate the cable being kept taut at all times so as not to foul the pulleys. This is especially important if upper car is fully laden and lower car empty - as is usually the case at the end of the day - when there is the maximum imbalance between the weights of the cars.

In the rare instance of an emergency stop being made on the tramway, the cables have to be checked before restarting to ensure that no fouling has occurred. At night both cars on the upper section run slightly further than they are permitted to do during the day and enter their respective car sheds at Summit and Halfway. On the lower section, with one car in Victoria Station the other is outside its shed at Halfway and at night has to be eased in by pulling the descending cable out of its conduit in a loop.

When the first section of the tramway opened in 1902, it was staffed by a station master, one winchman and six driver/conductors. This latter figure is an interesting one and suggests strongly that the intention – and certainly at least occasional practice – was to operate each passenger car (with a driver and a conductor) coupled to a van (with a conductor serving as a brakeman). Presumably some of the above staff also took care of maintenance. After the upper section opened staff numbers

60

increased and for much of the tramway's life it was worked by two winchmen or section engineers, four drivers, four conductors, two maintenance men, the booking clerk at Victoria and the General Manager – a total of fourteen, many of whom were employed only seasonally when the line was open. As has been the case with other British railways and tramways, one generation of employees has often been succeeded by another from the same families. From 1969 onwards the General Manager was replaced by an on-site Assistant Transport Manager, and with the introduction of one-man operation of the cars in 1990 (upper section) and 1991 (lower section) the conductors were dispensed with, though when the new Summit Station opened in 1992 a ticket-seller was employed there for the first time. At present, only four full-time staff are retained throughout the year.

Routine maintenance on the tramcars, the track and other parts of the tramway that cannot be carried out in the summer is done during the closed winter season and, before the line reopens each year, the cars undergo brake tests, laden with concrete blocks to simulate a full complement of passengers, as part of its official annual inspection.

SERVICES AND FARES

Like many other seasonal pleasure lines, the Great Orme Tramway's normal operating season extends from Easter through to October. (Early or late October – it has varied down the years.) This has always been the case – with the one exception of 1902 when it stayed open till the end of the year – in spite of the original expressed intentions of the Company to run a winter service for the benefit of residents along the lower section of the line. As was the UDC's privilege under the 1898 Act, it forbade the running of trams on Sundays until 1935; the principle of Sabbath observance was strongly held in the town during the early years of the twentieth century and the tramway was not alone in feeling the restriction. With the commencement of Sunday running the service was operated in an identical fashion seven days a week.

No hard-and-fast timetable has ever been employed on the

tramway for the very nature of the service and shortness of the sections make such regimentation pointless. Instead, the line has always been run to suit the demands of the season, beginning and ending with cars leaving the termini at a rate of three or four an hour and, at holiday peaks, eight cars an hour. (Similar variations can be introduced during a day's working if the weather or other circumstances render it necessary. Eight cars an hour is the maximum possible on each section, for the journey times are $5^1/_2$-6 minutes on the lower and $4^1/_2$-5 minutes on the upper. Hours of operation have varied little over the years, with services starting between 9.00am and 10.00am and finishing just before dusk; the actual time of the last car's departure has been scheduled at 6.00pm in recent years though sometimes late-evening running has taken place, again depending on the time of year (though never in darkness for road safety reasons).

Whilst the pattern of services has shown so little change, in contrast the scale of fares has altered considerably. Under the 1898 Act the permitted charges the GOT Co could levy (and not to be varied on Sundays or Bank Holidays) were fixed at 6d (2.5p) single and 9d (4p) return over the whole line. For shorter journeys the Company could charge as it thought fit - as it also could for invalid carriages or other special accommodation. A passenger's free luggage allowance was 28lb. Goods, minerals and parcels were to be carried, but livestock was excluded. The charges laid down in the Act for parcels were:

Weight	Cost
Up to 7lb	3d (1p)
Between 7lb and 14lb	5d (2p)
Between 14lb and 28lb	7d (3p)
Between 28lb and 56lb	9d (4p)

At an early date season tickets were offered for sale to residents, and to golfers using the summit course, the latter paying the princely sum of 15s (75p) for the privilege. In August 1906, at Lord Mostyn's instigation, additional single fares were introduced for the benefit of residents: these were 1d between Victoria and Black

Gate, and 2d between Victoria and First Station (Halfway), both applicable in either direction. A similar 2d fare was introduced at the same time for the trip over the upper section only.

Under the Statutory Undertakings (Temporary Increase of Charges) Act 1918, and the Tramways (Temporary Increase of Charges) Act 1920, the full single and return fares were raised to 8d (3.5p) and 1s (5p) respectively. These continued in force until 1934 when the new owner, the Great Orme Railway Ltd, discovered that as it was not a statutory company it had no legal power to charge them! The Great Orme Tramway (Temporary Increase of Charges) Order 1934 had therefore to be hurriedly obtained, followed by the Great Orme Tramways Act 1936, solely to authorise the existing fare structure. At this date the cost of season tickets was: week – 5s (25p); month – 10s 6d (52.5p); season – £1. In 1949 an increase in the standard return fare to 1s 6d (7.5p) was authorised by the Minister of Transport under the Defence Regulations, and in 1954 it was raised again, this time under the Transport Charges (Miscellaneous Provisions) Act, to 2s (10p), then again in 1965 to 2s 6d (12.5p). After this the fares continued to creep upwards until by 1972, following the changeover to decimal currency, the following scale of charges was in force:

Ticket	Cost
Victoria-Summit (single)	17p
Victoria-Summit (return)	25p
Summit-Victoria (single)	8p
Victoria-Black Gate (resident's)	2p
Victoria-Halfway (resident's)	4p
Children	Half price

Thirty years on, the fares for a journey between Victoria and Summit in 2002 were:

Ticket	Cost
Adult single	£2.95
Adult return	£3.95
Child single	£2.20
Child return	£2.80

A single fare of £1.50 was charged for a trip to Halfway – now the only intermediate station on the line with cars no longer stopping at Black Gate or Killen's Hill. (During the mid-1990s the only tickets sold were returns from Victoria to Summit, but the experiment proved unpopular and was later abandoned in favour of greater flexibility.) In addition, family and combined Great Orme Mines/Tramway tickets were available.

Finally, on a slightly macabre note, in the days when the tramway carried corpses to St Tudno's cemetery a charge of 2s 6d (12.5p) was made for the deceased. The mourners paid the usual fare.

Chapter Seven
ROLLING STOCK

The Great Orme Tramway is operated with a total of four passenger cars, this being all that is needed to work the two sections of line. They are numbered 4-7 and are the survivors of the original fleet of seven vehicles. Details of all seven are as follows:

THE PASSENGER CARS

These four cars, Nos 4-7, were built in Scotland by the Motherwell firm of Hurst, Nelson & Co Ltd, to the design of H.E. Taylor for Richard White & Sons. They arrived at Llandudno in two lots: Nos 4 and 5 were delivered to Llandudno by the London & North Western Railway in May 1902 and worked the lower section from its opening that year while Nos 6 and 7 arrived in 1903 to inaugurate services on the upper section. The two pairs have worked their respective sections ever since, never – as far as it is known - ever having swapped places on the tramway.

Each car is essentially identical to the others with two 4ft wheelbase bogies set at 24ft 4in centres; the cast steel wheels are 1ft 9in in diameter and set on mild steel axles. On the bogies is mounted the 37ft-long body, made up of a 30ft saloon and two open, 3ft 6in-long end platforms; the overall width of the car is 7ft 6in. The bulkhead at the back of each end platform is glazed and has a sliding door to allow access to the saloon where the transverse wooden lath seats provide room for 48 passengers. The seats are arranged back-to-back on each side of a central gangway, abutting onto the roof supports. Above the waistline the sides of the vehicles are open between the roof supports and unglazed. A further 12 passengers are permitted to stand, though not (since the 1932 accident) on the end platforms. A wrought-iron combined buffer/coupler 12in in diameter is still mounted centrally at each end of the cars, with side chains formerly used for attaching to the vans (see below), though these have long since fallen out of use.

Unladen weight is approximately 6.5 tons, and laden 10 tons.

On the roof of each car are still mounted the two trolley poles formerly used to connect with the overhead communciation wire, it being thought that removing them might damage the roof. (Until 1999 one pointed in each direction along the car, but after one swung loose from its moorings and damaged the roofs and guttering of three houses on the lower section, the two ends were fastened together in the centre of the car.) When the system was in operation, the pole not in use when ascending or descending was held down by a hook on the roof canopy, though originally this was done by turning the pole back along the roof and tying it down with a rope to a cleat on the body below the centre window pillar. The hand-generator, telephone and bell – now all removed – were mounted on the driver's panel on the open end platform, with this arrangement duplicated of course at the other end of the car. A foot-pedal operates a gong to give warning of the tram's approach where necessary.

Over the years several minor differences have existed between the cars. No 4, as constructed, originally had only one trolley pole, centrally-placed. It ran in this form for the 1902 season but by 1903 had been equipped with a trolley pole at each end of the roof in a similar manner to its sister cars, presumably because it proved an unsatisfactory working arrangement. Nos 4 and 5 were originally fitted with curtains to provide passengers with some weather protection but they were removed after only two seasons' running, doubtless because of the decision to stop winter services. Oil lamps were also fitted to the cars, one at each end, for running at night (to warn other road users and to illuminate the interior) but this practice was soon abolished and the lamps removed, presumably again after winter services ceased. The two lower section cars also carry water tanks, operated by a pedal, for watering the track on curves to reduce wheel/rail friction, and are fitted with lifeguards on the lefthand side (ie that facing Tŷ Gwyn Road) as a safety measure.

The only other major change made to the structure of the cars occurred in 1990/91 when, with the introduction of one-man operation, side doors and deadmen's pedals were added to the drivers' platforms at the behest of the Railway Inspectorate, again for safety reasons, and the water tanks on Nos 4 and 5 repositioned at the upper ends of the cars.

THE VANS

In contrast to Nos 4-7, the history of cars Nos 1-3 is not as well documented as could be hoped for but enough is known to give a general picture of their construction and use. They too were built by Hurst, Nelson & Co Ltd, and delivered along with Nos 4 and 5; they were not passenger cars at all though but vans intended for carrying freight on the lower section, coke up to the winding house and fuel and other supplies to the hotel at the summit. For reasons unknown, they took precedence in the fleet's numbering sequence. All three were identical four-wheeled vehicles with an overall length of 16ft 7in. The bodywork consisted of a 9ft-long closed centre section and a 2ft 6in-long open platform at each end; width was 6ft 10in. An overall roof was fitted and double folding doors, 4ft 6in wide, provided in each side whilst the upper half of the end bulkheads were glazed with further doors here to allow access through the van. Centre couplings and side chains were similar to those on the passenger cars.

Company records suggest that *four* of these vehicles were actually delivered to Llandudno railway station, though only three ever reached the tramway where, it is believed, they were used to test the newly-constructed sections before public services began (and presumably to carry material up for the construction of the upper section and completion of the Halfway complex). In September 1902 the Company decided to to fit two of the vans with seats, at a cost of £6 per vehicle, and install two panes of glass in each side of the body - though it is not certain if the work was ever carried out.

Details of the actual method of working these cars have not, unfortunately, survived, nor has the history of their eventual disposal. Their quickly-acquired nickname of 'jockey cars' adds weight to the theory that they were hauled – or even propelled, uncoupled, in Snowdon Mountain Tramroad fashion – up to Halfway by the passenger cars and then manhandled either into the boiler house siding or round onto the upper section for pushing up to Summit. It is believed that two of the cars were scrapped quite early in the life of the tramway and the third converted into an open coke wagon to ferry fuel up to the boiler house before it was made redundant by the introduction of road vehicles. All three were recorded as officially withdrawn from service in 1911 but this date probably bears little relation to when they were actually scrapped.

The fact that the passenger cars were equipped with centre couplers and chains suggest that high hopes were once held of using the vans as passenger trailers in a regular tramway fashion (though on such a steep line this practice is unlikely to have found favour with the Board of Trade). The likeliest theory is that they were used to carry coffins up to Summit for burial in St Tudno's churchyard; this is in fact extremely probable since it would have been virtually impossible (and most undignified) to manoeuvre a coffin into one of the passenger cars, lacking as they did the benefit of side doors, and would also account for the decision to fit two of them with seats.

BRAKES

All four passenger cars have – or had – conventional mechanical wheel (shoe) and tramway-style track (slipper) brakes operated by two brake spindles and wheels mounted outside the dash at each end of the car; the former bore on the car's wheel rims in order to slow their rotation whilst the latter bore down onto the top surface of the rails to check the forward momentum. (The two lower section cars were equipped with slipper brakes from the start but those on the upper section cars were only fitted after von Donop had insisted upon it at his 1903 inspection.)

As constructed, Nos 4 and 5 also had the emergency brake acting on the conduit slot referred to earlier. This was automatic in its operation: if the cable snapped and the strain on the brake ceased then the weight of the car running downhill caused the brake jaws to be forced with increasing pressure against the sides of the conduit. It was an extremely effective brake and the tragic consequences of its removal have already been shown, and in 1934 these two cars were fitted with a new automatic brake in place of the old one. This was supplied by Walker Bros of Wigan and overcame the disadvantages of the earlier one by employing instead four skids with steel teeth which come down and dig into the paved surface between the rails. The brake is governor-controlled to come into operation at a speed of 25% above the normal, ie at 6.25mph. It is equally effective as the old system and is capable of stopping a car in half its length. It can also be applied by the driver, by means of another spindle and wheel on each dash, and is in fact now the second driver-controlled brake for use of the slipper brake - which relied for its effectiveness on 12in x 4in metal skids or slippers pressing against the top surface of the rails – would effectively take some of the car's weight off the skid brakes and the slipper brake mechanism has therefore been removed from these two cars.

The vans appear to have been fitted with wheel brakes similar to those on the passenger cars with, in addition, a primitive 'snag' brake comprising two metal bars, each 2ft 1in in length. One end of each bar was attached to the haulage gear under the van while the other end was formed into a hook; both could be hammered into the ground to hold the van at rest in one of the sidings at Halfway. (It has been suggested that this brake could also have been deployed to snag against the track sleepers in the event of a van running out of control – this seems extremely unlikely since if a van was coupled to the upper end of a passenger car, it would not have been able to run away even if the couplings broke and, certainly on the lower section of the tramway, the hooks would have had no sleepers to catch on to!)

LIVERY

69

Car livery was originally a very attractive deep (or mustard) yellow colour for the bodywork, with white roofs and white lettering on each side reading: GREAT ORME TRAMWAYS. The number of the car was repeated before and after the name, again in white. Ironwork and running gear was painted black. (On the jockey cars the number was carried on the dashes.) At an early date the body colour was changed to unlined royal blue which became progressively darker under successive coats of varnish as the years passed. (According to a correspondent who remembered the tramway during the period immediately post-World War I, there was a short period c1920 during which the two upper section cars carried a different dark, holly-green livery.) Interiors were brown, with white ceilings.

In 1962 Nos 4, 5 and 6 were stripped down and repainted a bright, lighter blue with black lining; No 7 was treated similarly in the following year. Roofs remained white, as did the lettering and numbers, while the ironwork and running gear continued to be black. In 1967 all four cars were repainted again, the lighter blue parts reverting to the former royal blue with the addition of cream above the waist - this colour scheme being that later adopted for the UDC's buses. Side lettering from 1935 onwards was GREAT ORME RAILWAY (with the car numbers carried on the dashes from then on).

In 1977 the cars were repainted for the 75th anniversary of the line as part of a job creation scheme, using paint donated by Dulux. After a short-lived experiment in which the lower body panels were painted ivory, these and the dashes became bright (Trafalgar or Orient) blue while the window frames were ivory; beading was picked out in light blue-grey with the metal work on the body painted black and that on the bogies silver. The old-style lettering now read GREAT ORME TRAMWAY – once again the tramway's official title.

The last change came in 1991 (Nos 4 and 5) and 1992 (Nos 6 and 7) when elaborate golden-cream lining was added over ultramarine blue bodywork, slightly darker than before, and the cars given names. These, painted centrally above the window spaces, are: *St Tudno* (No 4), *St Silio* (No 5), *St Seiriol* (No 6), and *St Trillo* (No 7) – all names, of local saints, formerly carried by North Wales coastal steamers. Some of the work on No 6 was carried out at the Council's depot in Builder Street, to which it had been transferred by lorry after the 1991 season closed, this being the first time any of the Great Orme cars had left the line.

Chapter Eight
INTO A NEW CENTURY

There comes a point in every railway or tramway's life when the ravages of time necessitate the renewal of certain key items of permanent way, buildings and equipment. When the line is an important tourist attraction, of a type on which the most stringent safety standards must apply and one which, by its very nature, receives more than its fair share of operational stresses and strains, then at some point a major overhaul of virtually every part of the line will be called for. The alternative would be closure.

For the Great Orme Tramway, that point in time was reached during the late 1980s, with the tramway's prospects looking bleaker than they had done for many years. Although some local voices – both within and without Aberconwy Borough Council – were raised in favour of abandoning the tramway as a financial liability, for many closure was an unacceptable option. An alternative course of action was proposed: find someone else to take over the responsibility for it and, as mentioned earlier, the line was accordingly offered for sale or lease. In 1988 it was announced that the tramway would be leased to Bolton Trams Ltd, a modern company involved with tramcar restoration, for a 21-year period at a modest annual rent, though it opened that season still under local authority control. (Three, more local transport concerns are also believed to have expressed interest in leasing the line: the Llandudno Cabinlift, the Snowdon Mountain Railway and the Fairbourne Railway.)

The 1989 season saw it still in municipal hands – and making a profit of £35,000 from 117,000 passengers – which is when the Council made an abrupt reversal of its policy and decided that its Direct Services Organisation, Grŵp Aberconwy, would make the most of this unique and priceless asset and take over the operation of the line – a decision perhaps not unconnected with the fact that the original 1898 authorizing Act did not permit the Council to lease the tramway! Furthermore, it would spend some £255,000 immediately in order to bring the tramway back into peak working

In past years the GOT has never been been marketed as strenuously as it deserves. This beermat from its 'Railway' period is a rare promotional exception.

order and, from the beginning of the 1990 season, it would commence a £150,000 refurbishment programme spread over five years, the Railway Inspectorate having made it clear at the time of its 1989 inspection that the upper section would have to close at the end of the season on safety grounds. (Following the Welsh local government reorganisation of 1992, the local authority is now Conwy County Borough Council.)

Improvements to the tramway, which reopened on 4 May 1990, were begun at once. The upper, and most critical, section was closed until 28 June to allow the railway construction specialists

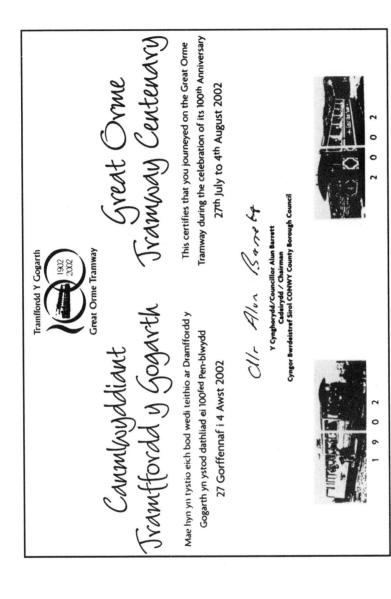

Tramffordd Y Gogarth

1902 2002

Great Orme Tramway

Canmlwyddiant Tramffordd y Gogarth

Mae hyn yn tystio eich bod wedi teithio ar Dramffordd y Gogarth yn ystod dathliad ei 100fed Pen-blwydd

27 Gorffennaf i 4 Awst 2002

Great Orme Tramway Centenary

This certifies that you journeyed on the Great Orme Tramway during the celebration of its 100th Anniversary

27th July to 4th August 2002

Cllr Alun Barrett

Y Cynghorydd/Councillor Alun Barrett
Cadeirydd / Chairman
Cyngor Bwrdeistref Sirol CONWY County Borough Council

1 9 0 2

2 0 0 2

The commemorative certificate issued to passengers during the line's centenary celebrations.

W. Hocking & Co Ltd, of Cardiff, to consolidate the embankment stretch, re-sleeper the track and repack the rail joints. In addition, new cables were installed. Despite this, there was a significant rise in passenger numbers to repay the Council's new-found faith in the line. As mentioned earlier, one-man operation of the cars was phased in during 1990/91, in order to made significant payroll savings – though at the same time the appearance of the line was improved markedly by the introduction of the current blue and golden-cream livery for the cars and matching blue uniforms, trimmed with gold, for the drivers. As also described earlier, a radio communication system replaced the old overhead wire link in 1990 – its introduction being precipitated by the breaking of one of the overhead wires that April! During the 1991 season the opening of the Great Orme Mines attraction that May led to joint ticketing and publicity arrangements, again in an effort to raise the profile of the line, with a free connecting bus service operated from Summit Station. It was to be the first in a series of ventures during the next few years combining a tram ride with a bus trip to another attraction.

The tramway reopened for the 1992 season with a host of improvements readily apparent to anyone familiar with the line. At Victoria Station the paved area had been relevelled and relaid with reclaimed York stone slabs, and a bayfront added to the booking office; at Black Gate traffic lights, tramcar-operated via sensors positioned beneath the track, now controlled the crossing and at Summit a new and spacious station building adjoined the (extended) Country Park Visitor Centre; this was officially opened on Friday 31 July to celebrate the 90th anniversary of the line, again with the Town Band enlivening the proceedings. The whole long weekend saw the issue of commemorative tickets by volunteer, on-board conductors from the Transport Ticket Society whilst during the week before, and the week after, the anniversary the trams ran until 9pm. At the same time an official guidebook to the line was produced for sale – somewhat surprisingly, the first time this had been done in the history of the tramway.

The very next year, disaster struck. On 10 June 1993, unseasonably heavy rains caused widespread flooding in the area, and the Great Orme did not escape lightly. The tramway was forced to close, while the staff could do nothing as surface water off the summit flooded through the cutting on the upper section and swept away the track ballast; other material washed off the hillside filled the conduits on the lower section with debris. Once again Hockings came to the rescue, and the line was able to reopen for business on 2 July.

Judging by the traffic figures, all these improvements and innovations – despite the odd setback – were paying off quite literally. In 1994 some 124,000 passengers were carried, and the following year this figure rose to 129,000 – a very healthy 4% increase. Although the hope had been to have completed the tramway's makeover by the middle of the decade, this proved impossible to accomplish, and plans for the last major reconstruction project – the rebuilding of the Halfway complex – had to be put on hold until all the necessary finances were in place. Then, during 1998, things began to move. That winter the Council spent £14,000 on renewing the entire track on the lower section – the first time this had been done since it was laid. At the beginning of 1999 it was announced that a £961,000 refurbishment grant had been approved by the Heritage Lottery Fund (to be matched by the Council with £786,000 of its own money). The following year the project was awarded £1 million of European Union Objective One funding, and a new, five-year refurbishment programme was put in place.

The first, £1.3 million phase of the refurbishment programme was the total reconstruction of Halfway. The opportunity to commence this came somewhat sooner than expected when, on Sunday 30 April 2000, the two cars on the upper section collided gently with each other at the passing loop. The cause, it was subsequently discovered, was the failure of the lower point and its inbuilt safety measures designed to prevent such a head-on collision. Of the 19 passengers taken to hospital as a precaution, thankfully only one was kept in overnight. Although a thorough inspection passed the tramway as clear to reopen after the defective trackwork had been replaced, the decision was taken not to do so. The two cars were instead placed in storage and a bus service substituted between Halfway and Summit; the following winter the winding engines were lifted out by crane for a complete overhaul. In the meantime, Halfway was transformed with canopies for passenger (and car) protection added to the front of each car shed, with paved areas laid beneath them for the benefit of alighting or boarding passengers. On an even grander scale, the two sheds were joined by corridors built onto their south sides to provide covered transfer facilities for passengers through a display area housed in a new, central structure complete with a viewing room for the winding gear, all beneath a glass-topper rotunda.

The scale of the work meant that the tramway did not reopen until July 2001, with the new Halfway Station not opening until 20 September. With Summit and Halfway completed, the next (and last) major task to be done will be the replacement of the lower section track. Commencing after the 2002 seasonal closure, the work is expected to take three years to complete.

In 2002, between 27 July and 4 August, the Great Orme Tramway celebrated the centenary of the opening of its first section with a week-long programme of fun events intended to recreate something of the atmosphere of that momentous day one hundred years earlier. The high point of the festivities came on Wednesday 31 July when, to the strains of the Llandudno Town Band playing 'Those Magnificent Men in Their Flying Machines' a special 'centenary tram' left Victoria Station, packed with guests and dignitaries on the first stage of their ascent to Summit where celebratory champagne and cake awaited. Trams and stations were bedecked with balloons and bunting, and some hundred staff and dignitaries (and crowds of onlookers) attended - many dressed in Edwardian costume. Among the guests were Betty Williams, the MP for Conwy, Alun Barratt, the Chairman of Conwy County Borough Council, and Mike Pearce, the Mayor of Llandudno, as well as numerous other local government members and officers. Each passenger that day – well over a thousand in all – was given a printed certificate as a momento of their trip, a complimentary glass of wine and a 'special Cententary birthday cake'; whilst souvenir tickets and certificates commemorated the occasion throughout the week.

Will such festivities will be repeated on 31 July 2102? Few, if any, of us will ever know for sure. One thing, though, is certain: if all the friends of the line have any say in the matter, the Great Orme Tramway is looking good for another hundred years of faithful service at the very least.

Acknowledgments

My researches into the history of the Great Orme Tramway began more than thirty years ago and it would be impossible, without fear of embarrassing oversight, to list all those individuals who have helped me in so many different ways over the years; so to everyone who did – thank you. I am especially grateful to those who kindly shared their memories of earlier ages of the tramway with me, to Jan for assisting with the photographs, and to Paul Smith and Margaret for their help with the other illustrations. I should also like to thank the staff of the National Library of Wales, and of the University College of North Wales Bangor, Llandudno, Birmingham and Cambridge libraries, and the staff of the former Caernarvonshire Record Office, for patiently assisting me in my attempts to unearth long-hidden facts and figures.

Finally, a special acknowledgment is owed to all the tramway staff who, throughout my long association with the line, have always helped make a ride on it such an enjoyable experience. This book is dedicated to them.

Possibly one of the first postcards of the tramway ever published, with car No 5 halted for the camera at the corner of Ty'n y Coed Road. The occasion may well be a pre-opening trial run, judging by the pristine condition of the track. The complete absence of buildings beside the road also indicates a very early date. (Photochrom Sepiatone Series, Author's Collection)

Another very early (though this time anonymous) postcard showing the Old Road/ Tŷ Gwyn Road junction and tramway crossing at Black Gate. (Author's Collection)

Car No 4 at Halfway on the tramway's opening day - 31 July 1902 - with the Company's directors and staff in attendance. The single, centrally-mounted trolley pole originally fitted to this car can just be made out behind the gentleman on the roof.
(Author's Collection)

Another early postcard, posted in 1905, published before the opening of the upper section, showing the engine house (but no car sheds as yet) at Halfway. The lower section cars are apparently running, with three other vehicles parked in the sidings –
see p99. (Author's Collection)

The rear of the original lower section car shed at Halfway in 1974, with the remains of one of the two tracks formerly linking the two sections of the tramway in the foreground. (Author)

Llandudno

Mountain Tramway II.

The GOT has been a popular subject for souvenir postcards ever since it opened and, with many views taken from the same vantage points, together they form an invaluable record of change on the tramway over the years. This one, posted in 1907, depicts car No 5 nearing Halfway in a very barren-seeming landscape. (Peacock Brand, Author's Collection)

The Great Orme Tramway, Llandudno

No 5 again, this time in Tŷ Gwyn Road, on a card posted six years later. The colourist has mistakenly given the car a reddish-brown, rather than the correct mustard yellow, livery. (Valentine's Series, Author's Collection)

An enlargement from a postcard of an upper section car in the cutting below Summit, very soon after the line opened for the car sheds have not yet been built at Halfway. Top right is a glimpse of the Conwy estuary. (Author's Collection)

Car No 4 in Tŷ Gwyn Road below the passing loop, probably c1920. The long sweep of the coast to the Little Orme is a recurring backdrop to the tramway on postcards of all periods. (E.T.W. Dennis & Sons Ltd, Author's Collection)

Car No 6 at the summit terminus, on a 1917-franked card, with the Summit Hotel beyond. The gentleman on the roof checking the trolley pole and its centre-body fastening is probably the driver, as the man on the car's platform is toting a conductor's cash bag and/or ticket machine. (Kingsway Real Photo Series, Author's Collection)

Although at first glance of little interest this card, posted in 1920, has been included because it gives a most unusual view of the tramway and, more importantly, shows the spot at Black Gate - just above the horse and cart - where car No 4 broke free to cause the 1932 accident. (Author's Collection)

Car No 5 at Black Gate - the actual gate is just visible behind the lefthand gatepost - on a 1939-franked card. Seven years earlier No 4 had careered down the hill at this very spot before leaving the rails, at the sharp curve beyond, with tragic consequences.
(E.T.W. Dennis & Sons Ltd, Author's Collection)

The fatal accident occurred on 23 August 1932; exactly three weeks earlier this card, showing the track down which car No 4 was to run away, was sent by a Mrs Parker to her son in Stamford. She begins her message: "Just a card to let you see where we went the other day it is terrible steep..." (Author's Collection)

TRAM ASCENDING THE GREAT ORME, LLANDUDNO.

The tramway in the 1930s and 1940s, as seen on postcards of the period. 1: Car No 5 climbing Old Road. (E.T.W. Dennis & Sons Ltd, Author's Collection)

2: No 5 again, this time in Tŷ Gwyn Road on a 1939-franked card, with housing developments now encroaching on the right. Just visible in the far distance is the coast of England. (Valentine's, Author's Collection)

3: Ten years on, car No 5 just below Halfway with the mountains of Snowdonia looming high beyond the Conwy estuary. (R.A. Series, Author's Collection)

4: *Car No 6 entering the cutting on the upper section with the boiler house chimney smoking merrily in the background...* (Author's Collection)

5: *...and near Summit.* (Valentine's, Author's Collection)

6: *An excellent view of car No 7 parked outside Summit Station car shed with the Summit Hotel - now minus its ornate canopies - in the background.* (Frith's Series, Author's Collection)

Three decades on, the tramway at work in 1974, before the recent modernisation programme was begun. 1: Car No 5 waits to depart from Victoria Station. The poster on the railings advertises day trips to the Isle of Man - a pleasure sadly no longer on offer today. (Author)

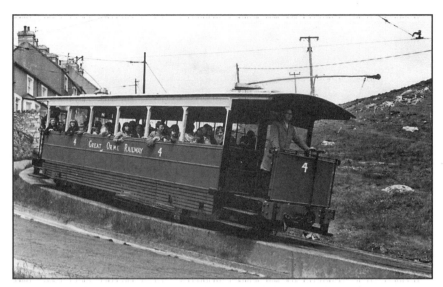

2: Car No 4 descending Tŷ Gwyn Road. As the car's livery proclaims, the tramway is still entitled the Great Orme Railway. (Author)

3: One of the old-style notices at Halfway, now replaced by more eye-catching signs. (Author)

4: One of the upper section cars in the cutting on the approach to Summit. (Author)

5: Summit Station as it was, with car No 6 in attendance. (Author)

GOT trackwork 1: The lower entrance to the lower section passing loop. Note the large gap at the junction of the conduits, covered when the tramway is not operating. (Author)

GOT trackwork 2: The upper end of the same passing loop, the point where the two tracks become - just - interlaced. (Author)

GOT trackwork 3: The interlaced track on the lower section, looking down Tŷ Gwyn Road. The haulage cables, and their supports and guides, are all hidden beneath the concrete paving. (Jan Dobrzynski)

GOT trackwork 4: One of the many original access covers on the lower section still in situ, bearing the main contractor's name. (Jan Dobrzynski)

GOT trackwork 5: In contrast, the cables on the upper section are completely exposed, as are their rollers and guiding sheaves. (Author)

GOT trackwork 6: One of the points on the upper section passing loop, showing the complicated arrangement needed to allow free passage of the cables.
(Jan Dobrzynski)

One of the standards, on the upper section, formerly employed to support the overhead communication wire but out of use since 1990. (Jan Dobzynski)

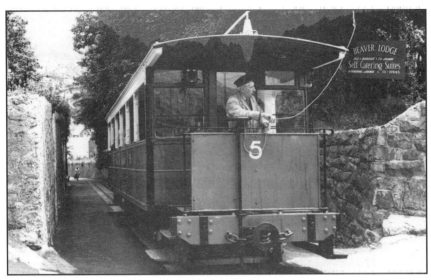

Communications, old-style: the conductor adjusts the rope controlling the rear trolley pole on car No 5 as it descends Old Road in 1974. (Author)

Communications, modern-day: the driver of car No 7 speaks to his winchman before setting-off from Halfway, 21 July 2002. (Jan Dobrzynski)

The passenger cars were equipped originally with curtains to protect their occupants from the rain, but these were soon discarded – though not before being captured on this "Autochrom" coloured postcard. As with the card on page 84, the car has been given a brown livery by the colourist. (Author's Collection)

Car No 4 in 1974 at Halfway, sporting the plain royal blue and cream livery of the period. (Author)

Sister car No 5, now named, on 21 July 2002 in its current, far more ornate livery (though the side panels appear to be in the middle of a repaint). Note the repositioning of the brake rods to inside the dash at the end of the car. (Author)

One of the upper section cars, No 6, displaying the full GOT livery, again on 21 July 2002. (Jan Dobrzynski)

The standard, utilitarian passenger car interior, the car in this instance being No 4.
(Jan Dobrzynski)

Photographs of the GOT's jockey cars are extremely rare, and of poor quality. This enlargement from the postcard reproduced on p82 depicts two of the three parked beside the engine house, together with an upper section passenger car (far right) not yet in service. (Author's Collection)

Close-up views of the brake controls at the upper end of car No 7... (Jan Dobrzynski)

...its coupling and buffing gear... (Jan Dobrzynski)

...and one of its bogies with its centrally-mounted slipper brake. The two axlebox covers identify themselves as being a 1901 original (left) and a 1932 replacement (right). (Jan Dobrzynski)

A closer view of the coupling gear. (Jan Dobrzynski)

A journey on the Great Orme Tramway in its Centenary Year. (All photos taken 21 July 2002.) Car No 5 awaits its passengers in the bustling Victoria Station... (Author)

...and loads up ready for departure... (Author)

... before setting off up Old Road past the King's Head. (Author)

No 5 nearing the top of Old Road... (Author)

... and about to pass into Tŷ Gwyn Road at Black Gate. (Author)

Still in Tŷ Gwyn Road, now above the passing loop. This time car No 4 is making the ascent. Note the slatted lifeguard on the near side of the car. (Author)

Car No 5 again, now leaving Tŷ Gwyn Road on the final approach to Halfway Station. (Author)

All change! (Author)

The new station building at Halfway, with its covered walkway on the left leading to the central rotunda. The station sign shown in the previous photograph is on the stone wall just out of frame to the right. (Author)

The upper section sign at Halfway, with the 1969 cabinlift above and beyond. (Author)

Halfway Station viewed from the upper section, showing the new overall roof (of Ffestiniog slates), the rebuilt car shed and the central rotunda beyond. Car No 7 waits to depart. The car sheds have been so designed that their other long-term residents – house martins - can still nest there. (Author)

From Halfway, virtually the whole of the tramway's upper section can be seen (and much of the cabinlift). In the distance, two cars are passing at the mid-way loop whilst Summit Station is just over the skyline to the left. (Author)

Descending car No 7 enters the upper section passing loop... (Author)

... and exits past the ascending No 6, all under the watchful eye of a maintenance engineer. (Author)

Car No 7 outside Summit Station, captured just after the start of its descent to Halfway... (Author)

... and, moments earlier, at the extended Summit Station, now with its covered platform area in front of the car shed. (Author)

With all the principal buildings now recon-structed or refurbished, the GOT looks in fine shape for the foreseeable future. This is the present-day Victoria Station, with its relaid platform area... (Jan Dobrzynski)

...and as seen from Old Road. (Jan Dobrzynski)

The new station building at Summit ... (Jan Dobrzynski)

...where cars can now load and unload... under cover. Long may they continue to do so. (Jan Dobrzynski)

One of the inspection pits in the rebuilt lower section car shed at Halfway...
(Jan Dobrzynski)

... and the new covered walkway past the winding house. (Jan Dobrzynski)